Praise for *Awakening the Sacred Body*

*"Tenzin Rinpoche has written an eminently practical, lucid, and inspiring guide to traditional Tibetan body-based meditation practices. These practices are designed to help us let go of the habits of mind that obscure our experience of the spacious awareness and wisdom that is our true nature. **Awakening the Sacred Body** is an excellent resource for new and experienced practitioners alike."*

— **Sharon Salzberg**, author of *Lovingkindness* and *Faith*

"I feel as if Tenzin Wangyal read my mind and body and then, in his kindness and wisdom, gave me clear, inspiring, accessible methods for integrating them. The insights, inspiration, and practices from this book offer so much support. This should be required reading for all those with an interest in yoga and meditation."

— **Cyndi Lee**, founder of Om Yoga and author of *Yoga Body, Buddha Mind*

"The wisdom tradition of Bön is yet another jewel from the spiritual treasury of Tibet. The Venerable Tenzin Wangyal polishes and presents it like a master jeweler, making it sparkle, delight, and give benefit. Read this book, work with it in a relaxed way, baby step by baby step, live with it, and your heart will open and your life will be way more fulfilling."

— **Tenzin Robert Thurman**, Jey Tsong Khapa professor of Buddhist studies, Columbia University; president, Tibet House U.S.; and author of *Why the Dalai Lama Matters*

AWAKENING THE SACRED BODY

AWAKENING THE SACRED BODY

TENZIN WANGYAL RINPOCHE

EDITED BY MARCY VAUGHN

HAY HOUSE, INC.
Carlsbad, California • New York City
London • Sydney • New Delhi

Published in the United States by: Hay House, Inc.: www.hayhouse.com®
Published in Australia by: Hay House Australia Pty. Ltd.: www.hayhouse.com.au
Published in the United Kingdom by: Hay House UK, Ltd.: www.hayhouse.co.uk
Published in India by: Hay House Publishers India: www.hayhouse.co.in

Design: Riann Bender • *Interior photos:* Janine Guldener:
www.janineguldener.com • *Interior illustrations:* Lhari-la Kalsang Nyima

The author of this book does not dispense medical advice or prescribe the use of any technique as a form of treatment for physical, emotional, or medical problems without the advice of a physician, either directly or indirectly. The intent of the author is only to offer information of a general nature to help you in your quest for emotional and spiritual well-being. In the event you use any of the information in this book for yourself, the author and the publisher assume no responsibility for your actions.

Library of Congress Cataloging-in-Publication Data for the original edition

Wangyal, Tenzin.
Awakening the sacred body : Tibetan yogas of breath and movement /
Tenzin Wangyal Rinpoche ; edited by Marcy Vaughn. -- 1st ed.
    p. cm.
ISBN 978-1-4019-2871-1 (tradepaper : alk. paper) 1. Yoga--Bon
(Tibetan religion) 2. Meditation--Bon (Tibetan religion) I. Vaughn,
Marcy. II. Title.
BQ7982.2.W33 2011
299.5'4--dc22

                                2010025565

ISBN: 978-1-4019-5554-0
Digital ISBN: 978-1-4019-2947-3

1st edition, January 2011
2nd edition, January 2018

Printed in the United States of America

CONTENTS

PREFACE

The particular teachings we will explore together in this book have helped me to move forward in my life, to deepen loving relationships, to expand creativity, and to support me in contributing more fully to my students and my lineage within the indigenous Bön tradition of Tibet. The meditation practices described within have been treasures for me and for my students. They are simple, direct, powerful methods suitable for anyone who is willing to reflect upon his or her life, and can support each of us to recognize and release familiar patterns that no longer serve while embracing the fresh and spontaneous possibilities available in each and every moment.

It is very important from time to time for each of us, as individuals, to reflect upon and take stock of where we stand in terms of our personal development, our commitments to our relationships and to our society, and our spiritual aspirations. When we are willing to look directly and honestly at where we actually find ourselves in life, the very limitations that we identify become the doorways to greater potential.

In society today, we elevate the status of our conceptual mind and seek change through our intellect. But how we experience the mind itself is a product of wind, or *lung*. (The "u" is pronounced like the "oo" in the word *look*.) In other Eastern cultures, *lung* is referred to as *prana*, *qi*, or *ch'i*. The mind's capacity for either subtlety and clarity or confusion and turbulence is all dependent upon *lung*. In the wisdom traditions of India and Tibet there is a vast knowledge about *lung* that has not fully taken root in the West. How can we have access to this wind? It is not through the conceptual mind, but through our direct, nonconceptual awareness. We access the wind by connecting directly with our body, our speech, and our mind—known as the three doors in both Bön and Buddhism.

I am particularly interested in how our relation to the internal winds can improve health of mind and body and bring change in one's own life and in society, ultimately liberating the suffering of cyclic existence, or *samsara*, altogether. Emptying samsara may be the larger goal, but emptying your anger toward your partner has immediate relevance. It is important that we work with our conditions as we experience them now. And in this work, wind plays a very important role in transforming suffering. I am confident that by deepening your understanding of wind, you will greatly enhance your ability to make important changes in your life.

I was educated in India as a monk in the Bön tradition from the ages of ten to twenty-five. I have great love and appreciation for my teachers and respect for my training, which was rigorous and unceasing. I have continued reflecting upon these teachings and bringing them into the life I now live as a husband, father, and teacher. In the past, I used to carry my books with me and read from them constantly. I have stopped doing that. It is not that I don't read at all anymore, but now I focus on bringing alive the teachings I have received and studied. This is what is challenging for me—to apply these teachings in all situations of life. This is the place where my life has energy, and this is the place from which I am inspired to write this book.

Life gives us so much opportunity to work spiritually. And I feel very thankful for the difficult situations I have encountered in my life because when I face something that is difficult and bring it to my practice, I can see real change. Every time I teach on these topics it is very lively for me. I am teaching them not as an expert but as one who is on the path. I feel that what I know is small, but the possibility to realize is vast. There is much of value in these ancient teachings, and as we learn to apply them, the creative possibilities of life present themselves ceaselessly.

I sometimes fear there is a danger of losing this precious knowledge that has come from a tradition of deep reflection and heartfelt commitment from teacher to student through thousands of years. I can already see how much has been lost from my teachers' generation to my generation. I can also see the possibility of what might get lost in the next generation, and so this also motivates me to bring this knowledge forward.

It is my hope that this book will guide and support you to explore and deepen your journey of reflection and transformation. Read it and engage in the practices with my blessings. May these teachings enrich your life and support you to clear what obscures you and to recognize your unique gifts so you may bring them into this world for the benefit of others.

Tenzin Wangyal Rinpoche
May 2010

INTRODUCTION

This is a book about personal transformation: how we, as individuals, can make positive changes in our lives; how we can transform or expand our consciousness, going beyond the limitations of prejudice and fear, beyond the bounds of familiar and habitual patterns to discover new solutions to the challenges we face.

In many forms of psychological and spiritual work, the mind is the focus. And it is not very easy to change the mind. Perhaps you are aware of having had good intentions that you were not able to realize. In our individual lives, there are many situations in which we feel limited by patterns and habits that we wish we could change, yet we don't know exactly how to do so.

You may have tried the common method of exerting conceptual power over yourself, basically a method of forceful advice. You reason with yourself: "I shouldn't do this. This is bad for me." You may have listed all the reasons that something is legally bad for you, ethically bad for you, or spiritually bad for you, and still you are unable to change. This is simply because many of our habitual patterns exist in a place deeper than our good intentions are capable of reaching, and so our intentions lack the power to effect the change we desire.

It is not uncommon in relationships that are facing difficulties that the parties involved declare positive intentions to each other: "Let's not fight. We'll have a nice dinner together, and from this evening on, we'll make a clear intention to not get to this point again. We'll talk to each other before we reach the point of fighting." So both parties agree and affirm this good decision and yet sooner or later come to discover that that decision did not prevent their next conflict.

In another example, perhaps a friend has done something and you are very agitated as you think of her behavior. "What was my friend thinking? How could she do this?" You may feel like you want to contact her right away and resolve the issue. Immediately you launch into strategies to solve the problem she created. You have an imaginary conversation with her in your head, or you sit at your computer and write an e-mail. Your intention is to clear this up. Perhaps your doctor, your spouse, and your friends have all told you that you need to relax, to let go, to not get so worked up over things—or for that matter, to simply not work so hard. Maybe you plan to go to the gym later, but right now you want to write an e-mail and clear up this conflict. Then you will be able to relax.

We often posit a "later" after we've finished certain tasks, when conditions will be better and we will be able to relax. But there is more available to you right now in the very midst of your agitation. Our agitation, conflicts, and habits can be the doorway to another dimension of being, an experience of clear and open awareness, vitality, and positive qualities.

Sometimes, when we are bothered by a problem, we think of the problem as being "out there." We externalize the problem entirely, and we simply conclude that the other person needs to change. Or when we try to fix a problem, we strategize and analyze over and over. Yet, as we mull over our challenges, our strategies and actions are driven by the energy of agitation and discomfort. No action that is driven by our discomfort will solve anything. It will only contribute to the problem. It is only when actions come from openness that true resolution is possible.

According to the wisdom tradition of Bön, by nature the mind is open and clear. This is who we are, fundamentally. Openness is the source of our being, and in openness we are connected to all of life. What obscures us from recognizing this source is similar to the way clouds obscure the sun. The sun is always shining, but from our vantage point—namely, our identification with our problems—we don't recognize the radiance. We are simply more familiar with identifying and dwelling on problems, and we're used to solving them with our conceptual mind. But it is through *nonconceptual* awareness that we are able to directly experience the mind's openness. The purpose of this book is to support you in becoming more familiar with the power of nonconceptual awareness, so that you can recognize the source within you and the positive qualities that flow from it.

How do we go from a sense of being stuck in our problems to accessing the open state of mind that is the source of positive qualities? When you want to make a change in a situation or in your own behavior, it is essential to shift your attention from the story you are telling yourself about what is happening to the *inward experience* you are having. The first place to draw your attention to is your body, to experience the discomfort and agitation directly. Your pain is the opportunity for transformation, and simply *being* directly with your pain will bring positive change.

How is this possible? By drawing your attention to your body, you can clearly feel the tensions and agitation that arise when you're experiencing something challenging. Sometimes the muscles of your abdomen are contracted or your jaw is clenched. You may notice that your breath is shallow or even that you are holding it. Your thoughts may be racing. We identify with our pain, making what is a product of temporary causes and conditions into something that is much more solid than it actually is. While not who you fundamentally are, identifying with your story and your reaction to it becomes a habit. Bön texts refer to this pattern as the *karmic conceptual pain body*. And this body is not by nature permanent or solid or fixed. Yet this limited experience of ourselves becomes an identity, a place of familiarity where we get stuck and spend far too much of our lives.

The structure of the karmic conceptual pain body is supported by what is referred to as wind, or *lung* in the Bön tradition. It is possible to shift your attention from the story that occupies your mind and connect with the very wind, or force, that holds the pain body together. Our moving mind actively produces all manner of stories and logic. This mind actually rides a wind, and when you catch this wind with your awareness, it can be guided. By connecting to the wind, it is possible to cause the dissolution of the structure of the pain body. Catching the underlying wind is like catching a horse, a horse that you can now ride in a positive direction.

Through focusing the mind and exercising the body and breath in specific ways, we can actually release the habitual patterns of the conceptual mind and, as a result, directly discover *being*. We can discover openness and recognize in that openness the opportunities for growth that we may have always wanted but lacked the proper skillful means to obtain.

In the yogic traditions of Bön there are many methods of working with the internal winds to transform our afflicting emotions (such as anger, attachment, and ignorance) into positive qualities, and transform our confusion into wisdom. By connecting with the internal wind, we catch the horse of the problematic mind and guide it in a positive direction. The wild horse of our internal winds can be tamed.

Usually when we have thoughts, we are aware of their content—what they are referring to. Thoughts are about things. We create stories with words and images, and react to these stories with feelings and sensations. Or we experience sensations and feelings, and create stories to explain them or worry about them. But if instead of getting caught up in the logic of the stories, you can simply become aware that you are thinking, it is possible to shift the focus from the content and to discover the wind, the momentum, or force behind thinking. Once you discover and connect with this wind, you can apply skillful methods to clear it and connect with the open space of the natural mind. And having connected with openness, many more possibilities are available to you.

It is important to emphasize the distinction between the conceptual mind and the nature of mind, which I refer to as open awareness. We do not need to think in order to be aware. And awareness is not thinking. Sometimes people from Western culture identify awareness or intelligence with thinking. This is not what I mean by the words *awareness* and *openness*. Open awareness means recognizing the fundamental, ever-present natural mind, which is clear and open like a light-filled sky. This state is natural to each of us, and the path of meditation leads us to recognize, trust, and become increasingly familiar with it.

We may start out spinning in the dilemma of a problem, mostly involved with what is "out there" and the story we create about it. But we can then bring our attention directly to our breath and our body sensations and begin to sense the energy behind the story. The energy behind the story actually has a structure, an energetic structure that you can become aware of. This energetic structure, or wind, is what we are referring to as the horse. This is the horse that you can catch and guide. We use the ordinary, or gross (physical), breath as a vehicle to guide the attention to release its fascination with content and to connect directly with the structure of our obscuring thoughts, feelings, and sensations. In the exercises in this book, again and again we will practice shifting our focus from a sense of problematic situation or relationship or challenge to connecting with the underlying energetic structure of that challenge. As we work with holding and then releasing our breath through various movements and with specific focal points, we can release the energetic structure of our confusion as we breathe out. We will learn to guide our breath through a subtle architecture in the body consisting of channels and chakras. Guiding and releasing the breath in this way, we are supported to glimpse the clear and open space of mind.

As we have noted, it is this clear and open space that is the actual nature of mind. This is the source of all positive qualities in life. Recognizing and becoming familiar with this source is the purpose of meditation practice. As we recognize and become increasingly familiar with the nature of mind, this enables us to experience a more joyful and beneficial existence. It is simply because we do not recognize and trust our natural openness as the powerful source that it is, and therefore do not live and act from this place, that our good intentions lack the necessary power to overcome our negative habits and we fail to actualize our potential in life.

All the meditation practices in this book guide you to catch the horse of your habitual patterns, to harness this internal wind by bringing nonconceptual attention to your breath, and to use this attention and breath to move the internal wind so that you can recognize your natural mind. The nature of mind is unmoving and clear—it is unchanging. It is also the unceasing source of all happiness and positive qualities. In the meditation exercises introduced in this book, we are moving the clouds that obscure the sky of the natural mind with the wind of our breath, uncovering a more subtle awareness that recognizes the nature of mind, the source of being. We all have this source within us; it is simply obscured by our thoughts and afflicting emotions. So it is only by habit that we do not recognize the source within us. We are distracted. While it seems that all humans seek peace and happiness, we constantly look outside of ourselves for this fulfillment, trying to secure our peace and happiness in conditions that cannot, by their very nature, be relied upon and that will inevitably change. This change causes further insecurity and dissatisfaction. We go after what changes and fail to recognize the deep and abiding inner space of being that never changes.

The wisdom teachings of Bön work with three opportunities, or doors to liberation from suffering: body, speech, and mind. In this book we will focus upon the door of the body. In order to attain liberation through the door of the body, we must focus on releasing the winds that support the karmic conceptual pain body and connect with the subtle internal winds of the changeless *essence body*, the subtle winds that support the recognition of the natural mind. As we explore working with the internal winds, it is my sincere hope that you will find much medicine for your life.

Using This Book and Online Video

In the following chapters, I describe the Nine Breathings of Purification and the *Tsa Lung* Exercises and how we might work with them in order to transform ourselves and our relationships. After reading about each exercise, you may wish to pause and watch and practice along with the online video. In this way, you can become more familiar with the particular movement and bring what you have been reading and reflecting upon directly into your experience in a deeper way. This is the traditional Bön way of progressing on the path: reading or hearing the teaching, reflecting upon what you have read or heard, and then bringing what you have understood directly into your meditation practice.

CHAPTER ONE

THE NINE BREATHINGS
OF PURIFICATION

The rider—the mind of innate awareness—
Is mounted on the horse of mindfulness.
Propelled by the wings of the unimpeded wind,
It moves through the path of the bodhicitta central-channel and
Arrives at the secret door of bliss at the crown.
The king of innate awareness nakedly arises.
Concepts—the veil of the intellect—are removed.
The self-arising primordial wisdom sees its own face.
Ignorance—the darkness of delusion—is lifted.

We have spoken of the nature of mind, referred to as the
natural mind, as being clear and open. It also is pure and without
fault. One who fully realizes this nature is referred to as a buddha, or *sangye* in Tibetan. *Sangye* is composed of two words: *sang*,
meaning pure, and *gye*, meaning perfected. Since the natural
mind is already pure and perfected, when we speak of purifying
the mind, it means clearing that which obscures the recognition

of one's pure and open nature of mind. Purification as a process releases the patterns that obscure the recognition of the natural mind and culminates in the recognition of the nature of mind, which is wisdom. The definition of *wisdom* is the recognition of the nature of mind. *Perfection* refers to all positive qualities—such as love, compassion, joy, and equanimity—which arise naturally and spontaneously as the result of abiding in open awareness. The source is openness, and the awareness or recognition of this openness is referred to as union, a union that gives birth all positive qualities. Perfection is not something to strive for as in the saying "Practice makes perfect." You already *are* perfect; it is a matter of recognizing openness and dwelling there, being there, and trusting this source within you. Positive speech and actions will arise naturally and spontaneously from this place of being. While you may think enlightenment is a long way off or a lofty ideal, it is actually right now, in this present moment. To think it is anywhere else is delusion.

Trusting and becoming more familiar with the power of abiding in the present have very practical applications in our day-to-day lives. Our anger obscures our capacity to love, our sadness obscures our joy, our prejudice obscures our equanimity, and our greed obscures our compassion. These positive qualities are fundamental to us. Even hearing this truth can loosen the grip of the mind's tendency to get caught in a seemingly solid world "out there" in which we are endlessly trying to find something or to fix something, and instead, can help us to turn the attention inward to connect with and to trust the true nature of mind.

The traditional goal of the path of meditation is to attain complete liberation from suffering so that one can be of benefit to all beings. And while this is the long-range goal, as you engage in practices taught in this book, I encourage you to look very closely at the life you are actually living. Reflect upon your relationships with yourself, with your family and friends, and within your professional life. Consider your life as a citizen of this world and reflect upon your contribution. These are the arenas in which you want to see changes in a positive direction. Any meditation done with the intention to benefit other beings should certainly benefit the people you live with and see on a daily basis. This prevents us from hiding out in spiritual practices or simply being caught in theories or fascinated with abstract principles.

OVERVIEW OF THE PRACTICE

The Nine Breathings of Purification, a meditation technique that has been practiced for thousands of years, uses the body as the means of connecting with one's natural mind. Basically, the practitioner takes an upright posture that supports wakefulness and imagines a simple, sacred anatomy of three channels of light within the body. After reflecting upon the presence of the challenges in one's life, the focus is brought to the inhalation as the breath is imagined moving through specific channels in the body, held slightly, and then released with the exhalation. As the practitioner releases the breath through a specific channel, subtle obscurations are released, facilitating the recognition of openness. After nine successive breaths, the practitioner rests in open awareness, bringing clear attention to the openness itself and connecting to this source of all positive qualities.

What follows are the practice instructions for the Nine Breathings, after which we will explore the instructions in more depth.

PRACTICE INSTRUCTIONS

The Five-Point Posture

1. Sit on a cushion on the floor with the legs crossed in front.

2. The spine is upright and aligned.

3. The chest is open, with the elbows slightly away from the body.

4. The hands rest in the lap, four finger-widths below the navel in the position of equipoise: Bring the thumbs to the base of the ring fingers. Place the left fingers upon the right fingers with the palms up.

5. Draw the chin inward slightly to lengthen the back of the neck.

It is acceptable to sit in a chair if sitting on a cushion presents a physical problem. The legs should cross at the ankles while your spine is upright and aligned, free of the support of the back of the chair. Everything else is as described above.

The Eyes

The eyes may be closed while performing the Nine Breathings to facilitate concentration. After the final breath, rest the attention in openness. At that time, open and rest the eyes in the space in front of you, gazing slightly downward.

Connect with Stillness, Silence, and Spaciousness

As you settle into the posture, connect for a moment with the stillness of the body, the silence of speech, and the spaciousness of mind.

Visualize the Three Channels of Light

Visualize, imagine, or feel three channels of light in your body. The central channel begins four finger-widths below your navel, rises straight up through the center of your body, and opens at the crown of your head. It is a channel of light, radiantly blue like a clear, sunlit autumn sky. Imagine the diameter of this channel to be like that of your thumb. There are two additional channels, one to the left and one to the right of the central channel. They have diameters slightly smaller than the central channel, more like that of your smallest finger. On your left side is the red channel; on your right, the white channel. The three channels come together to form a junction four finger-widths below the navel. While the central channel opens at the crown, as the side channels approach the crown, they curve forward under the skull, pass behind the eyes, and open at the nose—one at each nostril. The white right channel opens at the right nostril and represents male energy and method or "skillful means"; the red left channel opens at the left nostril and represents female energy and wisdom.

While connecting with the three channels of light, continue to settle into the posture and rest in stillness. Listen to the silence. Connect with spaciousness.

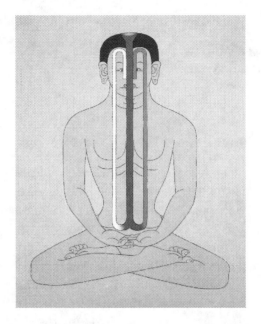

The First Set of Three Breaths:
Clearing the White Right Channel

Selecting: Bring to mind a fresh experience of anger or aversion, or become aware of the simple tendency to push your experience away. Imagine this; feel it; connect with it in your body, emotions, and mind.

Releasing: Press your right ring finger to your right nostril and slowly inhale pure, light-green air through your left nostril. Imagine that this breath follows the path of the red left channel to the junction. Hold the breath slightly here as you switch the finger over to press the left nostril closed. Following the pathway of the white right channel, breathe out slowly and gently at first and then more forcefully at the very end of the exhalation. Feel that whatever you have connected to releases through the right nostril with the exhalation, dissolving into space. Repeat this cycle for a total of three breaths, noticing the space that opens up as the white channel clears. Maintain a connection to the openness as you bring your attention to the red left channel.

The Second Set of Three Breaths:
Clearing the Red Left Channel

Selecting: Bring to mind a fresh experience of attachment; holding on; or the simple tendency to fill the space, to fill the silence with chatter.

Releasing: Press the left ring finger to the left nostril and slowly inhale pure, light-green air through the right nostril. Follow the path of the white right channel to the junction and hold the breath there as you switch the ring finger over to press the right nostril closed. Exhale slowly, gently at first and then more forcefully at the end of the exhalation, imagining that the breath moves through the red left channel, clearing the channel and dissolving the disturbance of attachment into space. Repeat this cycle for a total of three times, noticing the space that opens up as the red channel clears. Maintain a connection to the openness as you bring your attention to the central channel.

The Third Set of Three Breaths:
Clearing the Blue Central Channel

Selecting: Bring to mind a sense of disconnection, self-doubt, or lack of confidence. Let the experience be fresh. See without judging or analyzing; just connect with the raw experience.

Releasing: Breathe in fresh, pure, light-green air through both nostrils following the pathways of the side channels. Bring the breath to the junction. Hold slightly, and then breathe out slowly from the nostrils while imagining the subtle breath moving up the central channel, clearing the channel. At the very end of the exhalation, pull slightly in with your diaphragm and breathe more forcefully, imagining that you expel the obstacles through the crown of your head where they dissolve into space. Do this for three continuous breaths, feeling increasing opening or openness in the blue central channel.

Conclusion: Resting in Openness

Resting: Feel all three channels—right, left, and central—more open and clear. Draw attention to the center of your body, and be centered in that openness and clarity as you breathe gently and normally. To cultivate some familiarity with the experience of openness, simply rest your attention in open awareness. Abide. Don't plan the future; don't dwell on the past; don't change the present. Leave it as it is.

This concludes the instruction for the Nine Breathings of Purification. Next we will explore in more depth some of the principles that will make this practice useful in our lives.

PRINCIPLES OF PRACTICE

Posture

Taking an upright posture supports wakefulness. When the spine is straight, it brings the channels into alignment. Sitting cross-legged supports a subtle quality of warmth. If you are sitting on a chair, even though you cannot be cross-legged, cross your feet at the ankle. The position of the hands in the gesture of equanimity helps to equalize and balance the mind. Bringing the chin slightly in to lengthen the back of the neck helps to control thoughts and inner speech.

Inner Refuge: Stillness, Silence, Spaciousness

To successfully engage in meditation methods that support positive change in your life, to truly transform your confusion into wisdom, you need to connect with the healing space of being. The first step in the process of transformation is to shift from your allegiance with the karmic conceptual pain body, or your identity as a person with a problem, to an allegiance with openness. Simply put, you are moving closer to your authentic self and further away from your ego.

Right from the beginning, just be still in your body. By being still, you will feel directly whatever you are experiencing in your body in the moment because you are not moving away from it. You might become aware of discomfort or agitation. Stay with it. Just be with it directly. Experience your body. Every moment of connection to the stillness of your body is a moment of healing. This is something you can do throughout the day as well as something you do when you first sit down to meditate. Stop. Be still. Feel your body. If you are able to be still, you are entering through the door of the body rather than exiting, moving out, disconnecting from yourself through distraction and agitation. With practice, you can discover the inner refuge of stillness.

Next, draw your full attention to inner silence. Listen to the silence. Interestingly, when you listen to the silence, the sounds around you may become quite vivid. Your internal chattering may become more obvious. Let everything be as it is. Without struggling with anything, just continue to direct your attention to the silence, and you will discover a deep reservoir of peace. You are entering open awareness through the door of speech. Your inner dialogue will actually quiet on its own. This is also something that you can try during daily activities. Simply stop and listen to the silence. With practice, you can begin to trust that the inner refuge of silence brings you closer to who you are.

Finally, draw your attention to the mind itself. If you are engaged in thinking, stop and look directly at the thoughts themselves. In dzogchen, the highest teachings of Bön, there is an expression: "Observe nakedly." Just bring naked attention to the moment. Rather than rejecting thoughts or elaborating on them, you simply allow them, because they are coming anyway. Basically, you don't do anything. Just look directly at a thought. You don't reject a thought; you open to it; you go toward it, close to it; and as if trying to catch a rainbow, you go through it and discover spaciousness. A thought cannot sustain itself; it goes, and you discover the internal spaciousness of mind.

To support a sense of connecting with the internal space of mind, sometimes it is helpful to gaze at the sky. Just go out and look at the open sky. As you connect with the external openness, feel that same openness within you.

It is often very difficult for people to not continue elaborating their stories. Each person has very good stories. But if you bring pure attention to the mind itself, this pure attention discovers that the mind itself is empty. That is its nature. So even if it is just for a moment, connect with pure awareness, with the spacious open mind. In this way, you enter openness through the door of mind. Instead of exiting through the door of the mind by thinking,

thinking, thinking and disconnecting from yourself, you enter through the door of thought-free awareness or spaciousness and discover this powerful inner refuge.

In connecting with stillness, silence, and spaciousness we use three different doors but arrive at the same place—pure, open presence. Simply by connecting in this way, you are already transforming the challenges of your life instead of contributing to them.

Selecting

If you succeed in connecting with stillness, silence, and spacious awareness, you are in the right space to reflect upon a recent challenge or disturbance in your life. Invite that disturbance into awareness. Connect with it directly. Because your body is still, and because you are aware of that stillness, you connect more fully to what you are feeling. Feel any tensions, agitation, or emotions that are present. When we are not able to experience the stillness of the body, we are not very conscious of what is happening in our bodies, and therefore we are not able to connect with our feelings directly. If we are not able to contact our emotions directly, we cannot connect with their structure, or wind, and there is no way to release or delete this wind. If you can feel it while being still, you have managed to select it. To use a computer analogy, in order to delete a file, we need to select it, to highlight it, and then delete it or drag it to the trash can. The stillness of the body highlights the "file" that you want to delete. It is important to maintain an awareness of stillness throughout this process. You don't want to lose that direct connection.

To select properly, we must connect in three places: body, speech, and mind. In the body, we do this in the field of stillness, conscious of our challenge. Having an upright posture supports us to connect with stillness while directly experiencing our confusion.

It is the same thing with speech, the second place of connecting. You listen to the silence. It is very powerful and peaceful. When you talk, winds are moving internally, and those winds are usually not very helpful in situations where you are experiencing confusion. When you become silent and you are aware of the silence, the internal winds calm. In that calmness, invite a challenging situation or disturbance into awareness. If you feel the connection to the wind of the disturbance in that silence, then you have selected properly. But if you are talking to yourself, then you have not selected properly. It is difficult to experience a deep sense of inner silence right away. However, in the presence of the chatter of internal dialogue, bring your attention to the silence beneath the chatter rather than to the content of the chatter. If we are not feeding the dialogue with our active participation, it will cease to distract us and we can experience more directly our underlying feelings and sensations rather than our thoughts and commentary about our experience. It is this direct connection made through silence that enables us to catch the wind of the disturbance and delete or release it with the breath.

Finally, we come to the mind. The mind needs to be in the spaciousness of pure, open awareness. That means taking a break from the ego. For a moment, don't worry about why you have this challenging situation. All such questions are in the mind. Since these thoughts are there, allow them to be there. Don't fight with your thoughts, and don't elaborate upon them. A famous line in the dzogchen teachings says, "Leave it as it is." From the beginning you didn't leave it as it was, therefore you became disturbed. So now you have an opportunity to leave the disturbance as it is so it can go. The nature of your disturbance is impermanent. So just leave it. In that space of pure awareness, you are able to connect with the wind that is carrying that disturbance. In the stillness of the body, you connect with the grosser wind of the disturbance; in the silence of speech, you connect with the middling wind of the disturbance; in the mind, with spacious, pure awareness, the subtlest wind of the disturbance is exposed.

Sacred Anatomy

In the Nine Breathings of Purification, we work with the three main pathways, or channels of light, in the body. This is a simple, sacred anatomy that will support you to focus your attention in a way that will allow you to connect with the wind, or underlying structure, of your obstacles and conflicts, guide their release, and discover a deeper openness.

Visualizing these three channels of light supports positive internal attention. Sometimes we focus internally and just find dissatisfaction or discomfort. "My back is tight. I can feel my sore knees. I have a slight headache. My thoughts are jumbled." Here, we simply draw our attention to the three pure channels of light: the white channel on the right, the red channel on the left, and the blue channel in the center. While there are many channels in the body, these three channels of light are the most important for the practitioner of meditation. The transformation of suffering into wisdom happens through these three channels. This is the core of our sacred anatomy.

Purifying the Three Root Poisons
Through the Three Channels

The three channels are the pathways. Wind, or internal energy, is the horse that travels upon the pathways. The rider of the horse is the mind. The destination is the recognition of the nature of mind—clear open awareness.

The Nine Breathings work with purifying or clearing the three root poisons—hatred, or anger; attachment, or desire; and ignorance. Ancient tradition believes that the three root poisons are not only the causes of all suffering but also the causes of disease as well. We will explore each poison in more depth later as we work with the specific channels.

In addition to causing suffering, the three poisons also obscure the subtle wisdom energies and positive qualities available to us. These three channels are the deepest places in your body where the subtlest form of your suffering and confusion can be found. If you are able to purify your confusion at this level, it will definitely affect your life as you perceive and experience it. When the white right channel is clear of our subtle tendency for aversion and pushing away our experience, it supports the expression of spontaneous, beneficial actions in the world such as actions of love, compassion, joy, or equanimity. When the red left channel is clear of the subtle tendency to fill the space or attach to things or thoughts, it supports the recognition of the wisdom of emptiness, the pure space of awareness. When the blue central channel is clear of the subtle sense of a separate self, the struggle of ego-identity releases and there is no sense of separation. When your channels are clear and flexible, they support you to recognize the nature of mind—to be awake, fully present, connected to all life, and vibrant with positive qualities.

The channels are a pure path to enlightenment. If the three channels are open, you have a sense of healthy spiritual well-being. If the arteries in your body are blocked, you get sick. If these channels are blocked, you may not always feel physically sick, but in the dimension of inner consciousness you are not well and you are not manifesting your full potential as a human being.

The process of healing has to do with the ability to draw your attention to awaken a connection to these channels, to awaken the sacred body. And as you perform the exercise of the Nine Breathings of Purification, bringing awareness to the breath and working with the three channels have both physical and mental benefits. Let's explore each of these three channels in more depth in order to understand how to connect to the practice in a personal and meaningful way.

Clearing Anger Through the White Right Channel: The spontaneous expression of love and other positive qualities in our lives is blocked by the root poison of hatred, or aversion. We commonly experience this poison as anger, irritation, or the tendency to reject our experience in some manner. Are you open to seeing how anger is present in your life? Not all anger is something that we are clearly aware of. Anger can become an accepted part of our existence, as if it were a given. It is even possible to feel that if you separate from anger, you don't exist, so you'd rather be angry than be nothing. Sometimes when you feel very strong anger at things in your life or at other people, then it is obvious, and you can clearly say, "I am angry." But at other times, you don't even recognize it; it is just a state of being. You just sit with the anger. You don't have to say anything, express anything, or even feel the movement of your emotions. It's kind of a solid quality that is living with you and around you. It is important to recognize the presence of anger at these different levels.

Being still and silent and connecting with the spacious mind can allow hidden anger and agitation to surface. It is quite possible that we learn to manage our lives by pushing things out of awareness to a certain extent. Sometimes our busy lives successfully keep discomfort at bay. So when you stop and connect with stillness, silence, and spacious awareness, the space that opens up allows things that were hidden to surface. When this happens, do not be discouraged. This is an opportunity to release something that has obscured other possibilities from emerging in your life. The point is not to dwell in confusion by looking at who made you angry or to explore all the details of a situation, or even to look at your own angry mind with an analytical approach. No. If you are able to observe nakedly, that observation has power—the power to dissolve anger. But often we are not able to observe nakedly. When we observe, we begin to analyze, judge, and criticize. From there we argue, we fight, we might even feel like hurting someone. We don't want to go in that direction. So the bottom line, very simply, is that when you are angry, instead of looking out, just look inward and draw attention to your body; connect with any sensations and feelings directly without further elaboration. This is what is meant by connecting with the wind of anger. Once you connect with that wind, it is possible to clear it through a simple breathing exercise. In a very short time you will be able to clear your anger, because you are working directly with the wind that carries anger.

I cannot overemphasize the importance of connecting directly with what you are feeling. When your observation is not naked, raw, and direct, you tend to just crank out thoughts. You think you are changing, you think you are developing, you think you are working; but actually there is no development, only thinking. You are in the same place, circling around and around. When the clouds are moving in the sky and changing position, it does not mean clouds are clearing. Some parts of the sky are getting a little break from some specific type of clouds, but the sky overall is not becoming free of clouds. By contrast, there is no doubt when there is the experience of the cloudless sky. When you feel clear and open, that is very different from simply moving things around or rearranging stuff in your mind. So when you recognize anger or anger-related qualities of mind, behaviors, or states of being, simply see this; be aware without judging or analyzing or explaining.

Even in a simple practice like this, there is resistance to connecting with anger. "Why do I have to think about my anger? I want to have a break from my anger. I eat healthy food, do yoga, and relax with nature; and I am practicing meditation to develop peace. Now you want me to bring up my anger?" If you react like that, you may not be looking at anger in the right way. Perhaps when you look at your anger, you horrify yourself and other people. You immediately end up blaming somebody else or yourself. Some people don't want to blame others, or they're afraid or confused, so they blame themselves. Others feel they have the right to point the finger; if there is anything wrong in their life, it has got to be because of somebody else. They constantly criticize others. It is also easy to become hopeless and look away from situations that trigger anger. This looking away is just another, subtler form of anger because we are rejecting our experience. None of these approaches is successful in releasing anger.

So we need to look at anger with new eyes: raw, direct, nakedly observing. The gap between having resistance and being open is not a big gap, but sometimes it can be a very long gap. Some people can take ten years just to get to that place of feeling comfortable about looking at things. When you look directly at a situation of anger, it doesn't mean you injure yourself or become agitated, criticize anybody, or bring a lawsuit. It simply means being aware. So, simply look at aversion or anger-related states of mind or conduct. When you are able to see such a state clearly and feel it in your body, breath, and mind, you are ready to do the breathing exercise of clearing the right white channel, the channel in which anger abides and obscures a deeper potential.

In the exercise of the Nine Breathings, you bring your right ring finger to close your right nostril. As you breathe in deeply and slowly, imagine you are breathing a healing quality of light-green air through your left nostril. Imagine that breath follows the path of the red left channel to the junction. When it arrives at the junction below your navel, hold your breath for a moment as you switch your finger over to the left nostril, and press your left nostril while you breathe out slowly from the right. As you breathe out, follow the pathway of the white right channel. With a little push at the end of the breath, imagine that the wind that carries anger is expelled from your right nostril and dissolves into space. Feel the clearing for a moment, and then switch your hand back, pressing the right nostril and inhaling through the left nostril. Repeat this whole sequence for a total of three times.

If you are just learning the practice, you may want to simply focus on clearing anger through the white right channel and repeat this many more times, in order to become more and more familiar with the process. Each time, be conscious of the issues of anger, angry feelings deep in your body, in your energy, and in your mind, or even the more subtle tendency to simply push your experience away. Then breathe deeply in through the red left channel, hold at the junction for a moment, switch your hand over, and release your breath, imagining that it releases up through the white right channel, clearing the channel and dissolving into space with the exhalation. Do this again and again until you are aware of a shift, and then simply rest, breathing normally while paying attention to the right channel. Can you feel some degree of opening or openness? Continuously keep the spine straight and hold the body's position as you connect with openness.

When you release the breath, it is possible to feel that something has moved, something has cleared, and something has opened up. When anger dissolves, a new space is available. As you become familiar with that space, you will discover that the space is not simply empty of anger, but has a quality of warmth. What produces the warmth is actually the union of that space and your awareness. Becoming aware of the space in which anger has dissolved creates a new space for love, compassion, joy, and equanimity. And these positive qualities *will* come. Be aware of them. When you know to be aware, you will see something.

Clearing Attachment Through the Red Left Channel: The red left channel is referred to as the wisdom channel. As such, the subtle energies that pervade this channel support the recognition of space and openness, the true nature of being. This recognition is the definition of wisdom, which is blocked by the root poison of desire, also referred to as attachment. Attachments can appear as addictions—whether to drugs or alcohol, to food, to work, or to video games. We can be addicted or attached to ideas and points of view. We can be addicted to having to be right, or we can even be addicted to feeling inadequate. Through our addictions we may be seeking pleasure and excitement, a soothing of our anxieties, or a reassuring sense of self-worth through identifying ourselves with particular ideas or activities. We may be trying to fill the painful emptiness we experience because we have never learned to recognize the positive sense of emptiness, the vast space of our being. We also experience attachment when we try to hold on to a beautiful experience or a sacred moment. According to the teachings, white clouds or black clouds obscure the sun. Whether you are hit on the head with an ordinary rock or with a golden scepter, the result is the same—pain. So we want to overcome the pain of attachment.

It is not possible to let go of all attachments unless you achieve complete enlightenment. But there are plenty of attachments that you *can* release in order to live a more fulfilling and beneficial life. It is certainly possible to minimize the painful experiences that result from attachment. This pain can be very obvious when you are in a love relationship in which you want to feel the bliss of attachment but not the pain of attachment. The moment you cross the line from a pleasurable closeness to an unpleasant dependency you feel pain. Have you ever said or heard someone say, "I love you *so much!*"? Whether it's you or your partner who is saying it, "I love you *so much*" can be scary to hear. You are probably not particularly scared of the word *love*. What really scares you is the wind that carries those words, the intensity of the energy behind the words. You are reacting to what kind of wind carries that expression "so much." That is what you are aware of; that is what you are afraid of.

Perhaps you feel that you need more space in the relationship or that you should give your partner more space: "Well, I want to give space to my partner, but I don't know how that will affect the relationship." Your awareness is weaker than your insecurity or attachment; you have a plan to allow space, but somehow the plan is not going the right way. "I'll give you space, but when are we going to see each other again?" "Yeah, I know you need space, but call me tomorrow." One day feels like one year. What do you do at those times? Catch the wind. Don't catch the person. Don't even look at the person. If you really want to look at something, just go to the park. Look at how many people are enjoying life in the absence of that person! Join the club! Kidding aside, instead of focusing your thoughts outward on the other person, draw your attention inward, and just feel what you are feeling. Try to find a better position of your body to support you in bringing clear attention inward. Internally you are talking a lot. There is self-talk that you are conscious of and talk that you are not conscious of, which we could call subconscious gossip. There are winds that you are aware of and winds that you are not aware of. So simply bring stillness, silence, and spaciousness to your experience.

Once you feel some connection to that wind—whether in your body or energy or mind—you have properly selected it. Then we do the breathing to release that wind through the red left channel. Bring your left ring finger to your left nostril and press it closed. Breathe in fresh air, imagining that air as a light-green, healing energy. Breathe deeply in from the right, following the pathway of the white right channel to the junction. Hold the breath for a moment, and then switch your finger over and close the right nostril. Expel the breath through the left nostril, clearing the pathway of the red left channel as you breathe out. As the breath dissolves, feel the wind of attachment dissolve into space. In the Nine Breathings of Purification, you repeat this for three consecutive breaths before moving on, but for the purposes of becoming more familiar with the channels and with releasing attachment through the red left channel, you may wish to repeat this many times until you feel a shift.

Each time you exhale, remember to connect with a sense of opening in the left channel. Draw your attention to that space; be aware of that space. That awareness is like sunshine. Sunshine gives warmth. Warmth gives rise to positive qualities. After the final releasing breath, allow your breathing to return to normal, and abide, or rest, with clear attention in the openness of the red left channel.

Clearing Ignorance Through the Blue Central Channel: After connecting with and clearing the side channels, we bring the attention to the central channel. Visualize it. Imagine its presence. Without trying to impose an image in an effortful way, just try to feel this central channel as if it were already there. Feel that there is a channel, or conduit, of blue light that moves through the center of your body, beginning below your navel and opening to the sky at the crown of your head. Simply by drawing your attention to this channel of light, you can feel centered and grounded.

Now we reflect for a moment on the root poison of ignorance. By *ignorance,* I am referring to something very specific—the lack of realization of oneself. What does that mean? According to wisdom traditions, our true nature is like the boundless sky with infinite light pervading it. *Light* refers to our awareness, which recognizes the open space of being. When we connect with the space of being, when we recognize this, we are fully connected to ourselves. We are at home. The space of being and the light of awareness are not separate but in union. An experiential way to express the union of space and light is to say *open awareness.* Open awareness is the source within. Connecting with the source within, one has a deep sense that nothing changes, nothing can destroy or shake oneself. This is our true refuge. From this, true confidence arises. All positive qualities, such as love, compassion, joy, and equanimity, arise spontaneously from that space and are not shaken or destroyed by changing external conditions.

We disconnect from this openness as we become distracted by thoughts and perceptions—the movements of the mind. Although thoughts, feelings, and sensations do not have to obscure the open sky of our being, in fact, we do become obscured. We become disconnected from the source within us, and we experience this separation as insecurity and doubt. We seek to reestablish security, but our focus is outer-directed. As we lose connection to that infinite aspect within us, we try to substitute that experience with something else, something external, and that is why we are always on a journey and always insecure. We look outward for what will make us stable. Basically, each of us searches to achieve some stability in life. There is nothing wrong with stability, but the problem occurs when we think that stability comes from causes and conditions outside ourselves. When we find something that supports us, we hope that stability will last forever, and we fear it will not. That is a form of double conditioning or being doubly lost, because you are guaranteed to lose any external support you find. Whatever conventional stability you find will inevitably be lost. This is the truth of impermanence. In a sense, you can say we are constantly seeking refuge in the wrong places. It is a misguided idea to even try to stabilize ourselves in this way; nevertheless, we work so hard to do just that! This attempt to secure ourselves is the product of ignorance—failing to recognize one's true nature.

Instead of only theoretically understanding this fundamental ignorance, let's direct attention to how it actually shows up in your life. How does disconnection from a truer, deeper self manifest? How does lack of trust and familiarity with clear and open awareness manifest? Most commonly it manifests as doubt and lack of confidence—doubt in your work, in your personal relationships, or in the way you experience who you are. A lack of self-confidence can also be experienced as fear and insecurity, which is a result of being disconnected from a deeper sense of self. Doubt can manifest as indecision or hesitation to move forward or say yes, or conversely, as hesitation to bring closure to something and move on. Where is doubt most noticeable in your life? Where does doubt interfere with the flow of your life? How do doubt and lack of confidence interfere with joy in your life, with creativity in your life? It is important to reflect and bring this into your practice.

First, establish a connection with stillness, silence, and spaciousness. Then, in order to reflect, you do engage the conceptual mind in the beginning of the process, but only minimally. Look back over your recent life and notice times during which you felt uncomfortable or uncertain or restless. Perhaps there is a relationship that is challenging to you or a situation at work you are avoiding. As you bring a circumstance or relationship to mind, shift your attention from the situation or the person and notice how you feel in your body. Notice any restriction in your breathing or tension you may be experiencing. As you bring your full attention to your experience, do so without judging the experience. There is no need to think or analyze further. Simply be with what is—in your body, then with your emotions, and finally your thoughts. If you connect directly without further elaboration, this is what I am referring to as catching the horse, or the wind, that the mind of doubt is riding.

How do you know what to choose to bring into your practice? Choose what chooses you! Listen to yourself. If you reflect on your inner speech, you know what you worry about. If you listen to your inner thoughts, it will be something that you often find yourself engaged with, something that seems to follow you around. If you look at how you act, you know what chooses you in terms of the body. Choose what chooses you. I am not suggesting that you review all of your reasons or discern whether your reasons are valid or not; that is not our interest here. We are trying to feel and connect with the horse of that doubtful mind. I have introduced this notion of catching the horse of your doubt. How do you catch it? First, be aware of a situation in which you experience doubt or lack of confidence; then, bring your attention to *how* you experience the doubt in your body, in your energy field, and in your consciousness at this very moment. Once you are aware of this, you are no longer concerned with the event. The circumstance is simply brought to mind to evoke the feeling.

Bring your attention inward to the feelings and sensations of your body, and maintain a connection with them. Be still in your body and silent in your speech, and connect with the spaciousness of mind. As you do that, the experience of doubt awakens. Because of being still, the seeds of doubt come to the surface and become more obvious; because of being silent, doubt awakens in your energy field or emotions; it awakens in your mind, coming to the surface because your mind is thought-free, without judgment and analysis. Through stillness, silence, and spacious awareness, everything comes to the surface and becomes very clear in order for you to breathe it out. The breath connects with your doubt, which is clearly on the surface and is not hidden or obscured by thinking or analysis.

Now you breathe in pure air through your nostrils and imagine that light-green, healing air is following the pathway of the side channels down to the junction below the navel. You hold your breath for a moment there. As you begin to slowly exhale through your nostrils, imagine that the subtle wind at the junction now pushes right up through the central channel, sweeping the wind that carries the doubt. As you breathe out, pull your stomach in a bit and breathe out a little more forcefully at the end of your exhalation. The wind of doubt is propelled into space as you imagine that your exhalation is expelled through the crown of your head. Physically you are exhaling your breath through your nostrils, but you imagine the energy, or subtle wind, moving up the central channel and shooting out through your crown, carrying the doubt with it.

To become familiar with the practice, you can repeat the process of selecting and releasing the breath through the central channel many times until you feel a shift. And when you notice a shift into openness, you rest there. Try to be very conscious of the entire process. See how clearly you are able to connect with the wind, or the horse, of your doubt and to release it with the exhalation, focusing on the release moving upward through your crown. As your breath releases, recognize a clear, fresh, open space. After many releasing breaths, let your breath return to normal.

The process of releasing your breath brings a feeling of opening and a state of openness as a result. Become conscious and aware of this openness. Even if it is just a glimpse, it is important to rest your attention in that space. It takes a kind of discriminating wisdom, a subtle awareness, to be aware of the space that opens up.

After you let your breath return to a normal rhythm, allow whatever openness you experience to expand throughout your body, throughout the field of energy, and into deep consciousness. As an obscuration releases, your recognition of this openness is like the sun in a clear sky. Your open awareness has a quality of warmth. Merge and become one with that experience, and rest there as long as it is fresh.

The Power of Nonconceptual Awareness

It is very common to reflect upon a challenging situation or relationship by thinking in greater and greater detail, looking for a cause to the problem or seeking a solution. Your thoughts may go something like this: "Doubt? I never particularly experienced doubt until I got involved in this relationship. She is so complicated. Now I doubt what I'm doing because she challenges everything I say and do, and I don't like to argue. I think she is too insecure. I'm not sure she trusts me. I want to help her, but I realize this is really her problem and something she needs to work on. Now that I have sorted that out, I feel so much clearer." This is precisely *not* the way to select anything! Basically any action, any communication, any journey the conceptual mind takes is *not* what is being referred to as selecting the wind of doubt and is definitely *not* working with the subtle wind that supports awareness of the nature of mind. Instead, bring the relationship to mind. This may bring up some discomfort. Notice how you feel this in your body, in your emotions, in your mind. You are not looking for a cause or source of the discomfort by following your thoughts about the situation.

Rather you connect with the experience directly and then use the practice to release that. The openness that you can discover as a result is what we call the *source*—in this case, the source of the antidote to your doubt.

Perhaps you are concerned about a problem and think, "I don't have time to do this kind of exercise. I have to deal with this very real person in the real world." The moment you are doubtful or conflicted about someone, what do you do? You look outward at the person or the situation and begin to analyze, reviewing the past and projecting into the future, making a list and organizing your plan of action. In other words, you create stories about what appears out there in the so-called real world, and then you engage with those stories, focusing your attention on them. Many times in this process you don't even have a real connection to your emotions, because you are not focused internally or aware of how you are feeling. You are constantly criticizing, judging, analyzing. After you engage in this way for a while, you look at yourself and what do you do? You say, "What is wrong with me? I can't believe I'm in this mess again." And you do exactly the same thing you were doing externally, except now you judge, criticize, and analyze yourself.

When you judge, criticize, and analyze yourself, you are not really feeling what you are feeling, and therefore you are not experiencing the wind. The problem is the same whether you are focusing outward or inward: you don't have a clear, direct connection to yourself.

To resume our analogy of the computer, we can look at three folders on your computer. One is called "anger," one "attachment," and another "ignorance." In each of these folders there are many files containing many different memories and stories. It is not necessary to open each and every file, because the core of any story can be reduced to anger, attachment, or ignorance. If you are trying to open all the files inside, is it helpful? Maybe you can say, "Oh yes, then I'll know more about myself." Does it really help to review all the details of your anger and hurt, or the injustices you suffered? Is it not good enough to know that you have ignorance, or do you really need to spend even more time doubting whether you should be with this person or that person? Can you resolve anything by going over and over the stories? The suggestion here is not to worry about all the files you have accumulated and certainly not to create new files with the same old story driving the action.

Consider this scenario: You know you have doubt; you see that it produces thoughts; and you know that because of your doubt, you become vague and indirect when you try to communicate with someone. You can see how your doubt affects your ability to communicate effectively. You also understand the basic instructions in clearing doubt in the practice of the Nine Breathings. But now, when you sit down to practice, your conceptual mind is still active: "I know that my partner plays a role in this. This is not just about me. I'm going to have to say something to him, or else I'll always end up doing all the work." That inner dialogue, that conceptual mind, has no real relation to the energetic state of the doubt. It actually obscures the underlying energetic condition. Don't allow yourself to go on and on. Don't continue the inner dialogue. Connect directly with the wind of doubt. It is only when you cease to follow the story line—*no matter how convincing it appears*—that you can connect directly with the feelings and sensations in your body, the field of energy of your breath, and the moving mind itself rather than particular thoughts.

Experiencing a moment of nonconceptual awareness in relation to a current situation is much more valuable than all the ideas produced by the moving mind. I'm quite sure that many people simply focus on the stories of the moving mind. They are not connecting with their experience directly, and they keep working for such a long time without seeing change, simply because they focus on the wrong thing to begin with. Instead of eating a nourishing apple, they create an apple in the mind and then assume that by eating that mental apple some nutrition will result. Obviously, no nutrition is possible when you are not eating a real apple. In the process of healing, a nonconceptual, direct relationship instead of a conceptual, indirect, disconnected approach makes a big difference.

We need to value the power of nonconceptual awareness in order to change things. Nonconceptual awareness is the basis of positive transformation, the transformation of confusion into wisdom. Nonconceptual awareness allows us to change, transform, transcend. All positive qualities come from nonconceptual awareness.

So whenever we talk about facing something, the ability to face our challenges properly is determined by our connection to nonconceptual awareness. Whenever we can empower that awareness, we will be able to meet our challenges successfully. Whenever the connection to nonconceptual awareness is weak and we solely rely on the thinking mind, we will have more problems.

Some people beautifully resist looking directly at their problems. They can create incredible theoretical explanations about things. In the end, they are one hundred percent able to avoid challenges in ways that are so elegant. Then there are people who express themselves with such emotion, so passionately, and yet, in the end, nothing changes. Sometimes we complain when somebody else judges us, but when it is we who judge ourselves, it is even more horrifying. We constantly judge ourselves in the name of self-improvement, yet the judging mind is not the mind that will ever know or understand the nature of mind.

A fundamental principle of Buddhism is that until you overcome your conceptual thought, you are not enlightened. You can never become completely clear through the analytical process, simply because the analytical mind is not subtle enough to experience the nature of mind. While it is possible to have thoughts and not be bothered by them, please don't expect to have no thoughts at all. It is delusion to expect that. Practically speaking, we can reduce our habit of completely identifying with our thoughts and thereby having our thoughts determine our reality. Your meditation practice addresses the question of how well you can live with thinking, neither suppressing thought nor being lost in it, so that your thinking mind does not drive you away from being fully present. If nothing interferes with your experience of the fullness of being, then thinking becomes an ornament of the space of your being and does not obscure or separate you from your natural state.

So the essential point is this: Connect with stillness, silence, and spaciousness, and then look directly at yourself. Feel what you are feeling in your body, in your speech, and in your mind. Connect in a direct, naked, raw way in the present moment. This allows you to catch the wind of the moving mind and release it, discovering the authentic nature of mind.

In the Nine Breathings of Purification, while it is important to make sure you are clearly and properly selecting what is to be deleted, when you are breathing out, don't worry about what you are breathing out. When you press the delete button on your computer, do you have to think about what you are deleting? No, you don't have to think about what is being deleted. It is the selecting process that requires more care. With the computer analogy, once you have selected and highlighted in the right way, you just have to press the delete button. Selecting properly is the key, because many times that is the place where we fail. How do we fail? For example, you begin to think, "I feel my doubt, but maybe some doubt is good? Maybe this doubt is useful?" You begin to elaborate. I'm not debating whether doubt is good or not, but right at that moment, in order to deconstruct the structure of that doubt, do not interfere by engaging your conceptual mind if you want to delete the doubt. The nonconceptual mind is able to process doubt. But when you judge or evaluate the experience, you bring in the conceptual mind. When the conceptual mind is brought in, the experience cannot be deleted. The conceptual mind is not able to delete anything, so it just stays there. You may even have done the breathing, but the experience is still there.

It is also important to know that you may not feel a complete release of your anger, attachment, or doubt on any given exhalation. But each time you exhale and release the breath, become conscious of even a slight opening or openness in the channel in which you are focusing. It is like wind moving in the sky dissolving a small cloud; as the little cloud dissipates, you feel a little more space. At the end of the exhalation, it is important to be aware of whatever space becomes available.

Each time we practice the Nine Breathings of Purification, remember the four phases of the practice: connect with stillness, silence, and spaciousness; allow your experience to arise and then select; perform the exercise and delete; be aware of the space and abide in open awareness. The instructions for abiding are to not dwell on the past, not plan the future, and not change the present. Leave it as it is. Simply allow everything to be as it is.

While the practice is called "Nine Breathings," it is perfectly acceptable and even recommended that you explore the practice using more than three continuous breaths in any given channel in order to clear that channel. This depends on the amount of time you have to practice and your recognition of and experience of the clearing that results. Additionally, while at first you may sit in open awareness for a short time, gradually increase the amount of time that you rest, or abide. The importance of abiding in open awareness cannot be overemphasized, but it should not be forced.

RESULTS IN PRACTICE

The awareness of openness is like the sun shining in a clear sky. If the sun is shining, there is warmth in the space. If there is awareness of openness in the central channel, there is warmth in the central channel, in the core of your being. When there is warmth in the core of your being, that warmth gives birth to positive qualities that flower internally and benefit your life.

The longer you are able to remain in meditation while being open and aware, the more you will feel the warmth of awareness in that open space. The more warmth you feel, the more chances that positive qualities will manifest.

As we release anger, we develop love and other positive qualities. As we release attachment, we connect with the inherent richness of our being. As we release doubt, we develop confidence. Confidence flowers as a result of becoming aware of and trusting the clear opening within you. Imagine sunshine coming through a window where a plant grows. The sun is not saying, "Please open the window. I need permission to talk to the flower. Maybe the flower does not want me to shine on it." The sun has none of those doubts, nor does the flower. The only requirement is contact. Through stillness, through silence, and through pure nonconceptual, thought-free awareness, you make genuine contact with the sky of your being. Your recognition of this inner spaciousness is the sun that shines. As you are able to increase the time of that recognition, of that contact—as you are able to abide, or rest, in that spaciousness—the flower of your being grows. The internal warmth of your clear and open awareness allows the flowering of infinite positive qualities in your life.

Of course, first you have to feel that inner space. If there are a lot of clouds, the contact is not easily made. When there is little contact, little warmth is available and the flower will not grow.

When you delete the clouds, the sky is revealed and true contact is possible. This is not something you produce or force. The open sky of your mind is naturally present. When you connect with this, when there is true contact—continue, continue, continue. As you continuously maintain the contact, the result grows by itself. You feel increasing confidence, which is the result of the amount of time that warmth has within that space. It is that simple. Confidence comes by itself, naturally. It is not produced through thinking more strategically or talking more skillfully or acting in a particular way. The result is never produced or forced but arises naturally and spontaneously.

The flower of confidence will come by itself when you have contact with the warmth that is the result of being aware of the openness in the core of your being. That is what has been missing all along. Being aware of the openness and developing familiarity with it is essential. We can all agree that inner warmth is a positive, wonderful feeling, and most of us would love to be more confident in our lives. But if you look at your life, you can see that you often long for and miss this quality of warmth all the while engaging in activity and busyness and thinking and analyzing and searching—all of which continues the sense of disconnection from the very source of the warmth you are longing for. Sadly, we become more familiar with being disconnected from ourselves than being in true connection with ourselves.

So again, after you breathe out and delete what you have selected in the practice, what you do next is just rest in that space. You draw attention to either an opening or a sense of openness. Rest in the recognition of openness. Recognition is important, but resting in that recognition is also important. If you don't rest when you delete, then you are talking and thinking. You have to stop talking internally, which is probably not that easy to do. In order to select properly, you have to stop talking. In order to delete, you have to stop talking. In order to experience the space, you have to stop your inner dialogue.

If by doing this simple exercise of the Nine Breathings of Purification you feel a greater connection with openness, know that the ability to make changes in your life will come from that openness. If you make decisions about changes you would like to make in your life and none of those changes take place, it is because they were made on the surface. They didn't come from a deep enough or subtle enough place. Releasing the wind that carries our anger, attachment, and doubt and drawing our attention to the space that has become clearer is how we connect with that deeper, more subtle energetic level.

If you know the mind is changeable, you can have influence over it and you are in good shape. But if you think the mind has some inherent solidity to it, this is a serious problem. You may be thinking right now, "You have no idea of the difficulty I am facing in my life." Of course, everybody says those things. It's nothing new. It's the same story. When you know the mind can always change, you don't give so much power to your inner dialogue, which is a blessing. You no longer lose your sense of being through the movement of your thoughts and the stories that you spin. Thoughts constantly move and change, but your sense of being does not. Our moving mind creates a changeable karmic conceptual pain body. Our true being is changeless essence.

As you continue to engage in the practice of clearing all three channels, through repetition and increasing familiarity, you will begin to trust the space of openness more and more. Your sense of refuge in stillness, silence, and spaciousness will deepen. Openness and the awareness of openness—the union of space and awareness—is the recognition of one's true self. This recognition reconnects you with a deeper quality of being, which is something that was lost. As you become more and more familiar with that space, you will feel warmth in that space. Allow that warmth to pervade your body, your senses, skin, flesh, blood, cells, sensory experiences, and so on. How? Simply be.

If you do this breathing practice for half an hour a day, in a short time you will be feeling much better. For one thing, even if just for a moment, you get an immediate break from your patterns! That is an amazing experience. In the beginning you may question, "How can this really help? This feeling is so intense. I've been this way for such a long time. How can breathing out do anything here?" It takes time to become familiar and trust in the experience of releasing through the breath, and to trust that openness is the safest and most reliable place to be. And the ability to shift a familiar pattern is difficult. I know it is difficult. But we need to be willing to shift our allegiance from the familiarity with our pain and our problems and begin to trust openness. Once you connect with openness, the joy of living life begins. From openness we are truly able to create and contribute to the welfare of others.

CHAPTER TWO

THE FIVE CHAKRAS AND THE FIVE *TSA LUNG* EXERCISES

You have been introduced to the subtle architecture of the sacred body with the Nine Breathings of Purification. We have been working with the three channels of light, exploring the processes of selecting and connecting to the wind of our challenges, obstacles, and obscurations, releasing the wind of our disturbances through these three channels, and discovering openness and increasingly subtle experiences of being. As you rest with open awareness in the space that has cleared, resting more and more frequently and for longer and longer periods of time, you will deepen your familiarity with and trust in openness.

There is a further elaboration of the architecture of the sacred body that can be useful to release restrictive patterns and discover our positive potential. Within the central channel there are energy centers. The Sanskrit word for these energy centers, *chakra*, and the Tibetan word, *khorlo*, both literally mean "wheel." In this book the term *chakra* will be used, as it has already been introduced into Western vocabulary.

The exercises in this book work with five chakra locations within the central channel: the crown, throat, heart, navel, and secret chakra (which is located four finger-widths below the navel). Each chakra hosts specific opportunities to release patterns that restrict our lives, and each offers specific opportunities to cultivate positive qualities. We release through focus, breath, and movement and cultivate through abiding in open awareness, through letting go and becoming more familiar with the space that opens up as a result. As we look to the space that has opened up rather than continuing to focus outwardly on a person or situation or inwardly on a problem or story, we can discover unique and subtle energies in these specific chakra locations in the body.

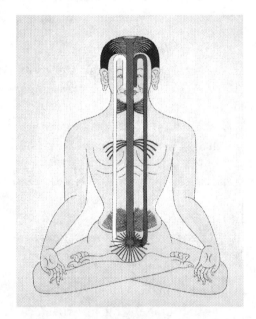

The Five *Tsa Lung* Exercises open the chakras in order to access the deeper wisdom that is always available. *Tsa* is the Tibetan word for channel, and *lung* is the word for wind, which we have been working with in the Nine Breathings of Purification. In these exercises, you inhale, bringing your focus and breath together to a particular chakra in the body. Then you reinhale and hold the breath and focus while performing a specific movement designed to open blockages and obscurations in that chakra. After releasing the breath, you rest in open awareness, which allows you to become aware of more subtle qualities. While the instructions for the exercises themselves are rather straightforward and don't take much time to learn, to practice effectively involves more skill.

THE FIVE *TSA LUNG* EXERCISES

1. Upward-Moving Wind

Clearing all the senses and opening the crown chakra,
Bringing forth the breath of bliss and the capacities of speech,
Causing the attainment of the ultimate, primordially pure body of truth,
From my heart, I praise the upward-moving earth-element wind.

The Upward-Moving Wind and the Crown Chakra: The first movement is the upward-moving *tsa lung* exercise. It clears both the throat and the crown chakras. Let's consider the opportunity that the crown chakra presents. Sit quietly for a moment and feel or imagine the presence of your central channel. Bring your focus up through the central channel to the top of your head, your crown. When we bring our attention to the crown chakra, energetically there is the opportunity to connect with boundlessness, the vast and open expanse of being. The nature of mind is always clear like a cloudless sky. Clarity is fundamentally the nature of mind, and openness is natural to all of us, but our natural clarity is often unrecognized because of habitual patterns of distraction. Upward-moving *lung* supports the experience of clarity. When subtle energies are awakened at this chakra, we may feel connected to all of life, for space pervades all of existence. On a concrete level, we may simply feel open, or approach a situation with an open mind.

As you bring attention to the crown chakra, connect with stillness, silence, and spaciousness. Then reflect on what blocks openness in your life. You may experience anger as one of the clouds that seems to block openness. Bring to mind a situation or relationship in which you experience anger, feel that cloudiness or agitation, become aware of it and select it properly, and then simply perform the upward-moving *tsa lung* exercise. At the beginning of the exercise, it is important to bring to mind a challenging situation or relationship in which you feel stuck. When you bring this to mind, you may feel your lack of openness as tension or agitation in your body, or experience a sense of anger, irritation, or fear occupying your emotional energy; you may feel distracted and overly active in your mind, or you simply feel dull and heavy. These conditions are held together by wind, and by being aware of this nakedly and directly without judging or elaborating, you connect with that wind. In this way, you select what will be deleted or released through the movement exercise. Having selected, perform the upward-moving *tsa lung* exercise as follows:

Upward-moving *Tsa Lung* Exercise: Assume a comfortable upright position, preferably the five-point posture or the chair position described earlier. After exhaling your stale breath, with your focus at your throat chakra, inhale a fresh, pure breath and hold it, imagining that your throat is holding the breath as a vase holds nectar. Without exhaling, inhale again, keeping a clear focus at the throat. Imagine that the focus and the reinhalation produce a certain

amount of subtle heat, which begins to spread and which you now guide up through the central channel to the crown by rotating your head five times to the left (counterclockwise) and then reversing direction and rotating five times to the right (clockwise). During the movement, feel the *lung,* or subtle breath, moving upward through the central channel to the crown of your head, cleansing and nurturing your sense organs and your brain. Now release your breath through the nostrils, slowly at first and then exhaling more sharply at the end by pulling in at the diaphragm. While expelling this outer, or grosser, breath through your nose, imagine that the inner, or more subtle, breath shoots upward through the central channel and releases into space through the opening at the crown of your head, carrying all obstacles with it. The obstacles release into the space above your head and instantly dissolve there. Allow your focus to rest in the openness at the crown, abiding there as long as the experience is fresh.

Each time you repeat the exercise, take time to select what you seek to clear, perform the exercise, and release the breath. At the conclusion, rest in open awareness. As you release through the exhalation, the *lung* goes upward through the crown and clears the block. You actually feel the movement of the *lung* going up, and the result is to dissolve the clouds of your obscurations in the sky of awareness. Whatever amount of opening you experience is significant. This is the process. Openness is the result that you feel. Recognizing and resting in the openness is key.

You can repeat the exercise three, five, or seven times, remembering to rest in open awareness for longer and longer periods of time as your ability to do so increases. Resting in open awareness is particularly important at the end of the set of three or more exercises before moving on to the next chakra.

The Upward-Moving Wind and the Throat Chakra: The upward-moving *tsa lung* exercise also clears the throat chakra, so you may repeat another set of three to five exercises focusing more attention there. Before beginning the exercise, bring your attention to your throat chakra. Reflect on the tendency to lie, or the tendency to speak sharply or to verbally attack someone with sarcasm. Or perhaps you are very good at spontaneously complaining. Perhaps you never speak your complaints out loud, but you make a face or purse your lips in judgment. Can you see those tendencies in yourself? Do you have experiences of them? We all do, but the question is how conscious we are of those tendencies. Sometimes negative speech can take the form of a simple comment to yourself about yourself, "Oh, I can't believe I did that again!" So first recognize that complaint. Recognize how amazingly spontaneous it is. You know you don't want to be critical, and yet you realize you are doing it anyway, even while you don't want to do it. Even if you do it a little bit better or a bit nicer, it is still a complaint. The energy of complaint is discernible. There is a wind supporting negative speech that is referred to as "unbalanced upward-moving wind" because it is so strong that you don't even have to strategize about how to complain. If you have to write a poem, you will sit and reflect, "How should I write this poem? Which word should I use here?" But a complaint just comes out. Some people do it very peacefully, in a soft and friendly voice, but still it is pure complaint. Others want the rest of the world to hear their complaints, so they raise their voices and shout loud enough for the neighbors to hear. Whatever the package, complaints are imbalanced upward-moving wind, as is lying, gossip, and slanderous speech.

Many of us like to gossip. Some gossip seems harmless, while other forms are more divisive and judgmental. You probably wouldn't want someone else talking about you in a certain way, yet when you talk about others, you may rationalize it: "We're just chatting over a cup of coffee. I'm not being harmful to anyone." Gossip is a curious activity. Some people really become awake when gossip gets "juicy." "It was so good talking to you. We have to do this more often!" You can see how a person's body wakes up and their eyes light up in anticipation. One sure way to put them to sleep is to talk about Buddhist awakening or the wisdom of emptiness or something like that. But fifteen minutes of juicy gossip and they will say, "I'm totally awake now!" This indicates there is some kind of familiar wind there.

Another challenge in the area of upward-moving *lung* is the ability to listen to others. Sometimes this is not very easy. Often one experiences the competition of one's own inner dialogue, so you end up actually listening more to yourself than to the other person. The lack of ability to listen and to see someone else clearly without bias is a form of wind that may involve afflicting emotions and certainly involves obscuring thoughts. These winds can be experienced directly by coming to stillness, silence, and spaciousness, connecting or selecting, and then deleting them through the upward-moving *tsa lung* exercise. In the resulting space that is clear, the ability to be present becomes effortless because you discover that this is a natural way to be.

Perhaps you recognize doubt as an obstacle that is currently playing a role in your life. What kind of doubt are you facing right now? If you want to make a change through the practice of meditation, your experience has to be current. It has to be personal. It has to be fresh. When working with doubt, you can look at the way it affects your speech. Your lack of self-confidence could result in poor communication. This could manifest as a lack of clear, direct, open, fearless, compassionate speech. Just imagine what kind of qualities are lacking in your communication with others.

You might say, "I am being direct!" That may mean your voice is strident, and you are yelling at somebody. That is not being direct. Rather, there is a little craziness there. You can be straightforward and say everything you have to say with a sense of open space and some kindness. But you may end up finding that you say something that you were not planning to say. You open your mouth and say everything that you did not want to say. And then you wonder, after you have said everything, "What did I say? I had a whole other plan of what I wanted to say, and I said totally the opposite." That is a block in communication. Basically, what is lacking is the recognition of open space. What does that mean? It means that at every given moment the experience of spaciousness is always there, but what is *not* there is your ability to connect with it.

So reflect on this whole area of speech: what you say to others, what you don't say but think, and the tone of your internal dialogue. See energetically if there is any way that you can feel some connection to that. Just be conscious of that, without judging. That is how you select what is to be cleared. Then, do the upward-moving *tsa lung* exercise again, this time focusing more strongly in the area of your throat and the feeling of the *lung* spreading and nurturing and cleansing your throat as you perform the exercise in the same way as before. As you release the breath through the crown, you delete what you have selected. Imagine the negativities dissolving into space.

Then bring your focus to the throat chakra, simply resting with clear attention in the space that is open at the throat. Resting in this way is the best medicine for cultivating positive qualities.

When speaking of the positive potential of the throat chakra, the analogy of the sun shining in the clear desert sky is used. The sun allows us to see the clear sky. A deep sense of completeness comes with the recognition of space. That feeling of completeness arises when the light of awareness meets space. The traditional analogy is the experience of a lost child recognizing her mother in a crowd—she feels complete in that recognition.

Experiencing the aliveness of positive qualities is related to the throat, but you may not be able to access those qualities because of your afflicting emotions and doubt. Often when you engage in gossip or complaint, you are separate from a sense of completeness. You may have seen that something is missing in your life, but you have lacked the knowledge that it is affecting a particular chakra or do not energetically know what kind of *lung* is causing it. What is missing is what we call clarity. These practices offer maps and tools to increase clarity.

The throat chakra is particularly suited to supporting awareness of the vividness of each moment, the fullness and completeness of being present. So after the obscurations of the space at the crown and throat chakras have been cleared, becoming aware of that space is like the sun lighting up the sky, illuminating the source of all positive qualities. It can be experienced as completeness. You are complete just as you are in this moment. Even just a glimpse of openness begins a powerful process that will eventually dispel the darkness of ignorance.

The role of the *tsa lung* practice presented here is to clear a specific symptom that you experience in your life. The symptom is like a cloud obscuring the clear sky of your being. You can clear that cloud away by using the upward-moving *lung*, with specific attention to what you are trying to clear, how you clear it, and where you are trying to clear the symptom. You are trying to clear what you are obviously aware of as the challenge or block in your life. How you are trying to clear is with upward-moving *lung*. Where you are trying to clear is in the throat and crown chakras. It is that simple.

Whatever issues you recognize in your life right now and are trying to work with in your practice might not be *the* fundamental key unlocking the door to your enlightenment. But these branches clearly have a connection to the root. You can make very direct and fast changes in how you experience your life by approaching your practice in the ways presented in this book. When you begin to see these changes, they become the motivation to engage further with the practice. Why? Because your meditation practice becomes a tool to work directly with issues affecting your life, issues that indeed have deeper roots. But as you continue to work, your awareness will go to those deeper roots. In the immediate sense, you will be able to clear some issues in order to experience more satisfaction in your job. This practice might support the survival of your relationship. It might be that the only way you can live life is to change a certain habit. Whatever challenges you experience in life are important to acknowledge and bring into your practice, rather than your practice becoming an escape from the challenges of your life. You want to experience spaciousness in the midst of the family dinner, not only when you leave the house to go on a walk by yourself. There are challenges in life that need to be dealt with directly and in a timely manner, and the practices presented in this book offer a way to do that. I encourage you to engage in the practices wholeheartedly and with curiosity, bringing your personal challenges to the practice and discovering the wisdom that lies within you.

Many of us can agree that there are times when it is obvious that we "just need some space." In our modern world, we often feel rushed as we go through the motions of our day; our mind feels overcrowded with responsibilities or the details of navigating life; and sometimes we are so exhausted by the end of the day that we just want to zone out with the television or a good book. While we may be theoretically able to entertain the notion that space pervades all form, even our own minds, we may not feel a connection to that space or recognize its presence in any way that is helpful to us. Through the use of the upward-moving *tsa lung* exercise, these experiences can shift significantly and dramatically. There is one tendency of mind that is important to notice, because it can undermine the positive effects of meditation, and that is our habit of moving from problem to problem. Without realizing it, we are addicted to our to-do lists or so much more familiar with our problems that we tend to dwell on them, even when we recognize that doing so does not solve them.

Through the clearing aspect of the *tsa lung* exercise, we release those physical, emotional, and mental habits, glimpsing a clearer and fresher state of being. Now the real practice begins—the practice of becoming more and more familiar with openness. Having recognized the lack of openness or spaciousness in any given situation, we become conscious and aware of it, select it properly, and use the breath and in this case the movement to delete it. We delete it in the right place to produce the right quality. In relating with the crown, we become more aware of space. That is what we are trying to do. Is this all really true? Does it work? We have to try! That is the fun part.

Even if you are saying, "Yes, I do feel clear, and then after a little while I go right back to thinking about my problems," that is a very good sign. Not a good sign that you go back, that is not the point, but a good sign that you do feel clear. It is a question of developing familiarity. We don't lack having the experience of openness, we lack having familiarity with the experience. We all have amazing experiences—glimpses of wisdom, joy, and love—but we don't have any stability in them. We feel so clear for such a short period of time. When we feel unclear, it lasts so long that it feels stable. So again, meditation is a process of developing familiarity with openness.

I want to clarify something about the metaphor of selecting and then deleting computer files. Please don't expect this process to be as easy as it is to delete files from a computer. "Okay, select it. Yes. Press delete button. That's it." I am using this as a metaphor to illuminate the stages of a process. When we are deleting, something is happening. For sure something has been deleted, but that does not mean all aspects of a habitual pattern have been deleted. You are on the way to wholeness, but do not expect that everything will be totally changed right away!

According to the ancient texts, as a result of the continued practice of the upward-moving *tsa lung* exercise, your mind becomes clearer and your ability to focus improves. Your speech becomes gentler and more peaceful, clearer and more effective, and it can serve to bring people together in harmony. The text even mentions that one begins to spontaneously sing and laugh aloud!

2. Life-Force Wind

*Generating the life force, which extends the
life span and opens the heart chakra,
Clearing thoughts and igniting the fire of wisdom,
Causing the attainment of the ultimate, spontaneously
perfected body of completion,
From my heart, I praise the life-force space-element wind.*

The Life-Force Wind and the Heart Chakra: Once again, bring your focus to the central channel of your body, using your imagination to feel its presence. Bring your focus to the middle of your chest where there is a center of energy called the heart chakra. Here the life-force wind resides. The result of the life-force *tsa lung* exercise is to increase longevity and strengthen willpower, memory, and confidence, which are all characteristics of the life-force wind. In the highest sense, this *lung* supports one's ability to abide or rest in the nature of mind.

Let's bring this into everyday life and explore how the life-force *tsa lung* exercise might be used. First, connect with the stillness of the body; listen to the silence; recognize for a moment the thought-free space of mind, a sense of spaciousness. Give this some time until you feel you have connected with this inner refuge. Your attention is in the heart chakra.

Now try to be conscious of a situation in which you feel a lack of connection with yourself. As a result of this disconnection, you may feel a sense of agitation, restlessness, and even anger; or you may become sad and depressed. Those are two sides of the same coin of being disconnected from oneself. As long as you have energy, then you get agitated and angry and act out. Then, when you lose your energy, you sink down and feel depressed. Of course, when you are like that, there is no enthusiasm or creativity, so there is no sense of willpower. Perhaps you experience a sense of sadness in life, of not experiencing the vividness or vitality that could be possible. You may feel dark, unclear, or stuck, with no movement.

We apply the same principle as we have throughout this book: bring this sense of lack of joy into consciousness, into awareness. See it. Even that piece can be challenging, because not everyone is able to recognize when they are disconnected from themselves. You become disconnected, but you are not able to see it. Sometimes we are not able to recognize this until we are involved in a frustrating or challenging situation or we notice that we are putting something off and avoiding something unpleasant. Our attention is dwelling on a so-called problem, but the source of this problem is being disconnected from oneself. So bring the attention back and look. The ability to do that is already a good step.

Having brought the attention back to oneself, the question becomes: in what way do you see? The instruction is to see what is happening without elaborating or judging. Do not judge what happened or what is currently happening or what has not yet happened. What we are trying to do is see what is there and see it in three locations: in the body; in the breath, or energetically; and in the mind. For example, in your body you might feel a sense of heaviness. Energetically you may feel nervous or agitated. Mentally you may feel easily distracted or experience unwanted thoughts. Perhaps you are not very clear about how you are feeling. I don't think it is a good idea to work too hard. If you are not clear, you are not clear, but if, in spending some time with your sense of disconnection you experience it clearly, work with that. Bring your focus either to this sense of not being clear or to whatever sense of agitation or depression is present. Again, this may not be something that you always feel. Perhaps it is only present as your weekend is coming to an end on Sunday evening. Perhaps you only notice it when you see a particular person at work. So bring the relationship or situation to mind, and then shift your focus and simply draw your attention to your body, to your energy, and to your mind. Pay specific attention to your heart chakra. Connect as clearly as possible without judging what is happening or elaborating further. Simply feel it. In this way you select, and now you begin the exercise to clear what you have selected.

Life-Force *Tsa Lung* Exercise: Assume a comfortable, upright position, preferably the five-point posture or the chair position described earlier. Place your hands on either side of your waist. With your focus at the heart chakra, exhale the stale breath and then breathe in deeply and gently and hold your breath. Imagine that your heart chakra holds the nectar of your breath, and as you take another short breath, a reinhalation, that nectar becomes warm.

Then guide the spreading of the nectar throughout the area of your heart while doing the following movements: Extend your right arm to the side with the fingers drawn together and circle the arm overhead, coming first to the front and then circling back and around to the side again. While you are doing this lassoing motion, you extend and spread the fingers and then close them again with each circle. Do this five times. Then repeat this motion on the left side, extending the left arm and bringing it forward and around in the lassoing motion, alternating the spreading and closing of the fingers and maintaining focus in your heart chakra. Continuing to hold your breath and focus, with the hands back in the position on either side of the waist, begin to move your upper torso and shoulder to the right five times and then to the left five times, exercising the heart area. Come back to the center position and release the breath through the nostrils. Imagine that the heart area is exhaling, releasing all the imbalanced wind, negativities, and blockages, which dissolve instantly into space. Rest your hands in the position of equipoise as explained in the description of the five-point meditation posture. (See page 4.)

Be aware of this physical sensation of opening, the energetic sense of opening, as well as any opening in your mind. Rest in the openness of the mind. Repeat this exercise for a total of three, five, or seven times, gradually increasing the amount of time you are able to rest in open awareness.

At the conclusion of the set, maintain your attention at the heart. The experience is open. Awareness is conscious of the openness. That awareness is like sunshine, so the more you are conscious of openness, the more warmth is brought to the space of your heart. The more warmth that is brought to your heart, the more you will naturally feel positive qualities such as joy. With the cessation of the negative obscurations, positive qualities spontaneously arise.

Awareness is the inner sun shining in the inner sky. The warmth of that sun will flower as positive qualities such as joy. Just continuously feel that warmth of the awareness in your heart. As you connect with the presence of any positive quality, allow the quality to pervade throughout your heart, imagining that it pervades through your flesh, through your blood, through the cells of your body, through your face, through your eyes. Allow the positive quality to pervade your expression. Physically feel those shifts and changes.

Consider the following metaphor. Imagine that the heart chakra is like a small garden with weeds and grass and stones representing your depression, your sadness, and your lack of clarity. When you look at yourself, you can see and feel that your positive potential is obscured, much like the overgrown garden. When you are conscious of this, you select it. When you are doing the physical movement, you are digging into the soil of the garden and clearing the weeds. When you are actually breathing out, you are removing those weeds. Now the soil is open and clear, and within it, seeds of the positive qualities are primordially perfected there. In dzogchen this notion of primordial perfection is known as *lhundrup*, which means that all positive qualities are primordially perfected in the space of being. For example, the seed of joy is already there. Since it is clear now, you can connect with that potential and see its expression coming out. So now you become conscious and aware of that clear and open field.

Your awareness is like water, sun, and air to the field of being, so the longer your awareness rests in that space, and the more you are familiar with that space, the more the plant will grow and flower or bear fruit. Unexpectedly you will see it. It is not something that you produce through effort. When it emerges, it is important to recognize it. Continuing with the analogy, as a gardener, once you prepare the soil and plant a seed, you care for the growth from shoot to bloom. In the process of meditation, taking care of it means, primarily, not elaborating or judging or changing anything, but being continuously aware. The longer the warmth of awareness hits that space, the faster the development. The more you are familiar with that space, the more stability you will experience. Once you have cleared the space, abide there.

Once joy manifests, there is no place for sadness because joy has expressed itself in form, and that form occupies the space that sadness needs. The logic is simple. The problem is doing it. The amazing thing is that there is often such a lack of trust in openness.

The next time you feel deep sadness, instead of trying to close the door, turn off the phone, cancel appointments, disconnect from the world, and go to sleep—and of course, people do those things—simply look in. Feel the sadness. Hold it in awareness while coming to stillness in your body, listening to the silence, and connecting with spaciousness. Do the exercise, again and again until you feel a shift toward openness. Then you can go to sleep from that open place. That's fine. That is a good place to go to sleep. When you wake up from that sleep, there is a very good chance you will wake up with a smile. So next time you experience strong or challenging negative emotions, just do the *tsa lung* exercise. Don't ask questions. Just be conscious and do the *tsa lung* exercise.

We always try to deal with the disturbed mind but not with what causes it, with the one who created the problem in the first place, with the fundamental cause—the lack of recognition of one's true nature. Imagine a room in which many people are gathered. When the sun is hot and the windows are closed and too many people are breathing together in close quarters, you may feel exactly what a depressed person feels. What will you do? Noticing you are not feeling very clear, will you say, "What is wrong with me?" If you keep on asking yourself that question for hours, you will feel worse and worse. You will exhaust yourself looking for your problem. And then at some point you think that maybe it is not you after all, maybe it is the person sitting next to you who is the cause of your discomfort, and you dwell on that for a while. You can even involve others in your speculation, making a phone call or sending a few e-mails. But the second solution will be to get up and open a window and let the air circulate. In a few minutes' time you can feel clear.

If I ask you which method of resolving the confusion you prefer, would you prefer the first one or the second one? Obviously the second one is more effective. It is the same thing with the heart. The heart needs fresh air. It needs the right kind of attention. It needs to be nourished with the awareness of the clear and open space of being, the space in which the subtle air moves and circulates, the subtle wind that supports the positive qualities such as love, compassion, joy, and equanimity. That is what it is lacking.

Attachment to Our Painful Identity: Let's say you are working with your sadness, and you have successfully cleared it through your *tsa lung* exercises. Those clouds are gone, the space is revealed, the sun is shining, warmth is there. Now what is available? It is joy. Why? Because the cessation of sadness opens up a particular space that births joy. In that very unique space, joy is underlying, waiting there, having merely been obscured by the clouds of sadness. So as the space receives the warmth of your awareness, the quality of joy emerges. When that inner space receives enough warmth, joy will manifest through you. Your structure actually begins to change. There is a noticeable glow in your eyes. You begin to see the positive potential in situations. Your speech begins to change, and you may find yourself spontaneously smiling or even laughing more. Your actions begin to change because joy has awakened in you.

But unfortunately, sometimes before joy reaches this place of ripening, you switch off. It is as if the electricity goes off. Maybe the connection has a short. Maybe there is something faulty with the switch. That's it. No more warmth. What has happened to the initial enthusiasm you felt in your meditation practice? Dissatisfaction is growing. You feel as if your meditation practice is no longer working. You have worked hard to clear something, but it seems like you are really more attached to what you are trying to clear than to what happens after clearing. "I understand my situation. I discuss it with my friends. We connect through our pain. In fact, I think suffering brings people together. My parents love me because of this pain. My support group loves me because of this pain. I even have a good relationship with my doctor because of this pain. What am I going to do if I don't have this pain? I'm going to lose all these beautiful relationships! My world will be empty." While this may seem a bit exaggerated, consciously or unconsciously we are afraid of losing what is familiar to us, even if it is pain.

Our attachment to our karmic conceptual pain body can become more and more subtle. Let's say that step by step, gradually you do overcome some attachment and suffering in your life. You have worked hard and managed to overcome some of your pain and confusion. But the moment you truly overcome it, you freak out. It is the biggest shock. "This is boring. There is no life here. I have nothing to say. I've lost my spark. There is no creativity." You may discover that your creativity, dialogue, and conversation all had to do with pain, so when the pain is not there, it stops everything. "I don't know what to talk about." In the silence of your inner space, you find no words. There is no other topic. Your conceptual speculations and pursuits have come to an end.

Why is this space not alive? This is a question about bringing life to that space. This is what we are talking about when referring to the warmth of awareness. Awareness of what? Of the space itself. Ten minutes of attention to the clear, open space of the heart brings warmth, and in that warmth, joy is ready to arise. When it arises, it is important to be aware of it. The awareness of the arising of joy accelerates or ripens the joy.

As I said, this is even reflected in our physical demeanor. Your skin, face, and eyes; the very structure of your flesh, blood, and cells, which previously expressed your sadness, begins to change. Your body is receiving a different message. When joy emerges in that space, a cycle is completed. Instead of manifesting your suffering, you now manifest your enlightenment.

When you do the *tsa lung* exercises, don't expect immediate and wonderful success. Expect that it will work. Expect that it might be challenging, but that challenge is nothing compared to your continuous engagement with confusion and negativity.

The very next time you get angry, realize that everything you want to say is called the "imbalance of upward-moving *lung*." So you now think: "Before it manifests in speech, I will release that wind into space." If it is going toward speech, do the upward-moving *tsa lung* exercise. But maybe it is not building in the direction of speech. Maybe it is more self-destructive in an internal emotional way. You get so mad at yourself, so disappointed, that you want to run away from the world. You feel so depressed, lonely, and deprived of support that you want to disconnect from the world and everyone in it. You are caught in your mind. So what do you do? Rather than dwelling there too long, work with your breath. Recognizing that the experience is very alive; do the life-force *tsa lung* exercise again and again. Connect with and release everything that you are feeling. Feel the underlying wind releasing from your heart.

Again, do not immediately expect to have a successful practice as described here. However, you *can* expect to go to sleep better. You *can* expect that your disturbances will lessen, but you may not see the flower of loving-kindness immediately. That may take some time. But each time you engage in the practice, you are preparing the soil. And each time you rest in whatever opening appears, you are nurturing that soil with warmth and moisture. So the seeds of loving-kindness, which are already present within you, will soon emerge. Giving your heart this attention is the place where you want to spend more time. As you clear more and more, paying greater attention to the space gives more warmth. As you continue repeating that for a few days, at some point you may even forget how terrible you were feeling. But don't think it is over yet. You must continuously practice. When you find the space, it is much more possible to warm that space, because of fewer disturbances.

So now that you have begun to warm that space, this is the point at which many mistakes can happen. You might start looking around for another problem, because that is what you are so familiar with. That is a mistake. What should you do? Instead, keep on warming the openness with your attention until the full expression of joy or love emerges from that space. The full expression of joy is some sense of confirmation that there is no sadness anymore—at least in that context, in that relationship, in that specific issue where it was previously occupying you.

Each of us has to question what it means to remain for a longer time in open awareness. For a yogi, every moment being in that space is being with God. So why would the one who is seeking to encounter God make that connection shorter? When you encounter God, will you say, "God, sorry, I have another appointment; I'd like a rain check"? If a child has become separated from his mother in a crowd and is seeking her, missing the love and contact with her, when he finds his mother, will this child say, "Oh, sorry, Mom, I'm actually kind of busy now"? For the individual who has lost a sense of self for years and years, and who finally finds a moment of a sense of authentic self, will this person say, "Sorry, self, I have another self waiting for me. You look like a real self, but I have another one who does not really look like a real self, but still I am a bit attracted to that one, at least for now. I'll go out and make a quick trip, but you wait for me here, please"? Would you say something like that? Probably not. So those are good reasons to become increasingly familiar with abiding, with resting the mind in open awareness.

3. Fire-like Wind

Digesting food, generating heat, and opening the navel chakra,
Nourishing the body's physical strength and
quickly igniting the heat of bliss,
Causing the attainment of the ultimate,
nondual body of emanation,
From my heart, I praise the fire-element wind.

The Fire-like Wind and the Navel Chakra: The next chakra location is the navel. This is where we connect with the fire-like wind. Fire-like *lung* has much to do with digestion, providing physical heat in the body and extracting nourishment from our food. When fire-like *lung* is not sufficient, we may not digest our food properly. But the principle of digestion covers a broad spectrum, from the gross to the subtle, from the fire that digests our food and provides nourishment to digesting the subtle veil of ignorance, resulting in the great bliss of the union of space and awareness.

Thoughts, emotions, and duality itself are all digested by the subtle heat of our awareness. These very thoughts block the positive qualities from fully emerging, so as these blockages release, the warmth of our awareness at the navel chakra ripens the positive qualities. As these positive qualities ripen, wisdom digests or dispels the darkness of ignorance; joy digests or dispels the heaviness of sadness; love digests or dispels the disruption of anger. Joy and love both have the quality of heat that digests our obscurations. Joy and love are important qualities in healing oneself. The heat of compassion burns self-centeredness and is essential in benefiting others. Joy and love and compassion are qualities that naturally arise from the union of space and awareness. In other words, when we have connected with a clear and open space within ourselves, when we recognize that space and allow it by giving it our attention, the seeds of love and joy and compassion are already present and will emerge when needed.

What blocks our positive qualities from emerging are our afflicting emotions of anger, greed, ignorance, jealousy, and pride, which often go unrecognized or are easily projected outward upon external objects and people. "That person makes me sick; I can't believe he could do that!" "My family is so materialistic; I can't stand to spend too much time with them." We are all familiar with the term "unfinished business" in reference to unresolved conflicts and tensions between people. Another way to understand this is as an emotional conflict that has not been properly digested. With the fire-like *tsa lung* exercise, we use the heat of our subtle *lung* to digest our afflicting emotions. We are not using the conceptual mind to analyze our problems, but we are using the powerful tool of our nonconceptual awareness.

Let's explore this a bit further. Reflect upon the relationships you have with people in your life. You may notice a relationship where there is a bit of stickiness. This can range from slight, barely noticeable discomfort to a more highly charged experience. Perhaps you experience this discomfort when you bring to mind an event or situation that occurred or is coming up in your life. This discomfort is the undigested emotion that can be brought to your meditation practice and cleared with the fire-like *tsa lung* exercise.

Bring your focus to the navel chakra and simply allow these feelings or sensations of discomfort to be present. By entering into the stillness of body, silence of speech, and the pure and open space of awareness itself, this discomfort is allowed to emerge more clearly. As feelings and sensations emerge, feel them directly in your body, breath, or energy; and see them clearly in your mind without elaboration or judgment. In this way, you have properly selected what is to be cleared. It is important that you allow your experience fully without judging it or rejecting it, or you will simply be meditating with the attitude of getting rid of something that you don't like. This is just another form of aversion or anger directed toward yourself, so it is important to allow even this discomfort fully into awareness in order that it, too, may be released. Next, perform the fire-like *tsa lung* exercise, as follows.

Fire-like *Tsa Lung* Exercise: Assume a comfortable upright position, preferably the five-point posture or the chair position described earlier. Bring your hands to either side of your waist. With your focus at the navel chakra, allow sufficient time to select what is to be cleared.

Now breathe in a nourishing breath and hold this breath at the navel chakra in the following way: pull up on the pelvic platform (the muscles that hold the pelvic organs in place), the perineum, and the anal sphincter. Press down with the diaphragm. This hold is called the vase retention. With the focus clearly at the navel, reinhale and feel a sense of increased warmth. Imagine that this warmth spreads and nourishes the navel area as you physically rotate your abdomen in a counterclockwise direction. Then reverse and rotate five times in a clockwise direction. Coming back to center, breathe out slowly through your nose, release the hold, and feel that the navel chakra is releasing all negativities. Imagine any conflicts or obstacles dissolving into space as your breath dissolves. As the physical and energetic sensations settle, become aware of the space that opens up within you, and rest your attention there. Gradually bring your hands back to the position of equipoise.

Repeat the exercise for a total of three, five, or seven times. After the final repetition, maintain your attention at the navel, resting for an extended time in open awareness. This attention to openness is the best medicine. Open awareness is likened to the sun shining in the cloudless sky precisely because when we are free of judgment, our awareness is nourishing, like the sun that nourishes all life. We are so used to our attention playing the role of a critical and judgmental observer. The *tsa lung* exercises enable us to let go of this judgmental observer, releasing our attention to rest in the clear, open space where the medicine of loving-kindness, joy, compassion, and equanimity are freely available.

If your fire element is very balanced, physically you are unlikely to experience digestive problems. In the energetic sense, you will digest or process your emotions better when you connect with internal energetic heat. The subtlest inner warmth supports a deep stability in one's capacity to abide in the nature of mind, enabling you to overcome duality altogether.

4. Pervasive Wind

Generating strength in all the limbs of the body,
Accomplishing effortless and spontaneous virtuous activity,
Causing the attainment of the ultimate essence body,
From my heart, I praise the pervasive wind-element wind.

The Pervasive Wind and the Junction of the Three Channels:
The next *lung* is called pervasive wind. The nature of this *lung* is to pervade throughout the body and beyond the bounds of the body. Pervasive *lung* is related to wind. Even though each of the five *lungs* has to do with wind, the pervasive *lung* is specifically related to the wind element. If you look at the nature of wind, wind moves.

Wind is communication. Having a balanced wind element is the opposite of being stuck.

When you feel stuck in life, you feel a lack of creativity or a lack of movement. Perhaps there is some sense of "I can't do it." You feel unable to handle something, to take the next step, to expand. You feel hesitant, impeded, or blocked in some way. Your movement is restricted. Perhaps you go to work and have a particularly stressful day. If you are successful with your pervasive *tsa lung*, you will not bring your stress home and will still be able to be open and loving with your family. The different roles that you perform do not interfere with each other when your pervasive *lung* is good.

Perhaps you are working at home and feel, "I need peace and quiet in this house! I need to work!" Everyone has to be silent because you are working. That is also an example of deficient pervasive *lung*. You know that your difficulty in working has nothing to do with the noise of your children or family. You are hearing your own noise. Yet when you go to a noisy café, you feel that the buzz of the café energizes your creativity! So you see, it is in your mind. Look at an area in your life where you may have these challenges, and bring this to your meditation practice.

When we feel anxious or agitated, our mind sometimes obsesses in one specific area. We may repeat to ourselves, "It's impossible. There's no way I can do that. This looks like it's going to be problematic." So we focus in a narrow way and many times repeat the same negative slogans to ourselves around the general theme that it is impossible. When you locate that internal territory and become conscious and aware of it, working with the body and energy and the mind through the pervasive *tsa lung* exercise will open up those boundaries and restrictions. Once they are opened, the energy flows and supports a natural sense of expansion in your life. This is a wonderful discovery to make. It is not that you lack creativity.

It is a little energy block that exists in you, and it does not remain a physical or energetic block, but becomes a mental block. When it becomes a mental block, the mind is not able to find a solution or enrich its creativity. When you open up your channels and chakras, this also opens up the mind. When this openness is recognized, the mind sees many possibilities.

Have you ever thought to yourself, "This coming week I'm going to work hard, but on the weekend I'll enjoy myself"? How about the phrase "I just have to get through this week, and then I can come up for air on the weekend"? What does that mean? Does that mean you are not enjoying life or that you are holding your breath until the weekend? We divide up our experience like that all the time. Even just saying to yourself, "I'm having a bad day," presupposes a solid experience that cannot possibly be accurate when you become more fully aware. Things are simply not as solid as they appear. And this is very good news, which we take full advantage of in the practice of meditation and of *tsa lung* in particular. We attack this apparent solidity and stuckness on three fronts: body, speech, and mind.

So the number one priority is to become conscious of your stuckness. Before you can change a pattern, you have to become conscious of it. When you become conscious of it, just for fun, flip how you describe it to yourself. Instead of, "Oh boy, today is going to be a tough day," how about saying, "I'm going to discover something new at work today"? Do it five or seven times before you go to your job and notice what happens. Of course, changing our patterns isn't as easy as that, but for sure it is not as difficult as you think. So whatever sense of limitation of concept and focus you discover, you can expand that and allow a fresh and more subtle wind, a pervasive wind, to move throughout your experience.

There is a potential for playfulness with the *tsa lung* exercises if you are willing to experiment. Suppose you are trying to accomplish something in an area in your life in which you are really interested, but you are fearful or nervous and lack confidence. Just look at those feelings and connect. Bring this sense of hesitation or restriction to consciousness; bringing it into awareness and selecting it properly are the same thing. Then release it through the *tsa lung* exercises. The blockages that you feel, you release. The potentiality that you feel, you expand. Even a slight thought of something being possible should be expanded; expand that positive seed. Dissolve the seed of doubt that you have; dissolve it simply and directly with the pervasive *tsa lung* exercise. You will be surprised how much it will affect you. Is it true or not? This is your experiment. You can find out directly through engaging the practice.

First, the point is to be conscious and to recognize that you have a question, experience a little doubt, or feel a block. That block might have a place in your body or in your emotions or it may be affecting your mind. Again, be conscious, select it properly, and then perform the pervasive *tsa lung* exercise to clear it.

Pervasive *Tsa Lung* Exercise: Assume a comfortable upright position, preferably the five-point posture or the chair position described earlier. Exhale the stale breath, and then inhale and bring your breath to the junction of the three channels, four finger-widths below the navel. As you reinhale, imagine that your breath enters the central channel, filling the channel from the junction to your crown, and then begins to expand throughout your body. Raise your hands up over your head and clap them sharply together, rubbing them to generate some friction and heat. Then, while imagining the subtle *lung* spreading throughout your body, quickly massage your body from the top of your head down, including your limbs. After massaging the body, continue to hold your breath as you make a gesture of shooting an arrow five times

to the right and then five times to the left. Feel a sense of expansion beyond the bounds of your body as you do this. Coming back to center, release the breath slowly and completely through the nostrils. Feel as if your entire body is exhaling through every pore. All your creativity comes out of that space. That is why that space is very valuable. All the energy of hesitation and constriction releases and dissolves into vast space. Do this exercise three, five, or seven times, always being conscious of what you are selecting to clear before beginning each repetition.

When you have completed the final repetition of the exercise, rest in open awareness, feeling present throughout your entire body, connecting with the fresh wind that supports positive qualities. After deleting a computer file, what do you do? You check to see how much space is available. It is not as if you delete files and then never pay attention to the space—you *always* have to pay attention to the space. So anytime you delete something, recognize that space.

5. Downward-Clearing Wind

Obtaining mastery in retaining the vital essence and expanding bliss,
Opening the secret path and igniting the bliss of one's own nature,
Causing the attainment of the ultimate body of great bliss,
From my heart, I praise the downward-clearing water-element wind.

The Downward-Clearing Wind and the Secret Chakra: Now we bring our attention to the secret chakra, located at the base of the central channel, four finger-widths below the navel. This is the chakra of action and manifestation, and in its enlightened aspect that action arises from the union of openness and awareness. This union is the source from which all positive qualities naturally arise and manifest, and our actions will be spontaneous and for the benefit of others.

What happens when this energetic center is blocked? On a physical level, we may experience illnesses related to the elimination processes of the body. The reproductive processes are also affected by the downward-clearing *lung*. The secret chakra has to do with one's sexual dimension, and attachment or desire is the obstacle that often blocks this chakra on an energetic, or emotional, level. Attachment obscures the recognition of the base, or source, within us, and through attachment we suffer from the emotional insecurity of being dependent on other people or addicted to substances for our well-being rather than connecting directly with our inherent well-being.

Blockage at this chakra also occurs when we force ourselves to do something that we don't want to do but have to because of work or family obligations. You can see how you struggle when your action is forced. Can you imagine the possibility of an action that is *not* driven, an action that contains joy and light? Recognize your resistance, your difficulty in that circumstance of forced action. Bring that sense of conflict to the practice, and be with it nakedly and directly. Select it and then perform the downward-clearing *tsa lung* exercise.

Downward-Clearing *Tsa Lung* Exercise: Assume a comfortable upright position, preferably the five-point posture or the chair position described earlier. Connect with stillness, silence, and spaciousness. Allow and select that which you are seeking to clear, and then assume the following position: Seated on the floor, cross the legs at the ankles, with the right leg in front of the left and the knees off the ground. If seated in a chair, you simply cross the right leg in front of the left at the ankles. Place your hands at the sides of the knees and feel this position as a stable base.

Exhale the stale breath, and then inhale a fresh, pure breath. Bring the focus to the secret chakra at the base of the central channel, four finger-widths below the navel. Hold the breath and pull up on the muscles of the anus, perineum, and pelvic platform. This hold, which differs from the vase hold because it does not engage the diaphragm, is called the basket hold. Maintain this hold throughout the exercise. Without exhaling, inhale again and turn to the right knee, clasping the knee with both hands. Rotate your pelvis five times in a counterclockwise direction. Then turn to the left knee, and clasping the knee with both hands, rotate five times in a clockwise direction. Come back to the center position with hands on either knee and rotate your pelvis five times counterclockwise. Throughout the rotations, maintain your focus at the secret chakra and imagine that the *lung* spreads, nourishing and purifying this

chakra. Slowly release the breath through the nostrils. Release the hold and feel that the release in the secret chakra flows downward like water. Feel the blockages and obstacles dissolving into space with the breath. Rest with clear attention in the secret chakra. Repeat this exercise for a total of three, five, or seven times.

Releasing and Cultivating: The purpose of the *tsa lung* exercise is, first, to release blockages in a particular chakra (in this case the secret chakra), to open it, and to feel clear in that chakra. Connecting with the clear and open space enhances your ability to connect with the positive quality that is needed in your life. As you maintain clear attention at that clearer place—clearer because of the release through the exercise and your awareness of the opening—this clear attention serves as medicine to heal conflict, pain, and confusion related to that chakra, not only to the sexual dimension of yourself but to the way you connect with your world altogether. Does your world seem to irritate, thwart, or block you, or is your world alive and inviting? Can you experience challenges as opportunities? Do you dance with your life? As you continue to explore the downward-clearing *tsa lung* exercise, you can realize the transformative quality of the downward-clearing *lung* and the opportunity of the secret chakra—to engage life fearlessly, with openness, awareness, flexibility, and joy.

We have been exploring the five outer *tsa lung* exercises. All five can be done as one session of meditation practice. It can be useful to complete a set of one each or three each of the exercises, and then concentrate upon one of the energy centers, spending more time focusing there, doing three, five, or seven repetitions of the exercise before resting in openness at the conclusion. Emphasizing a particular chakra in your practice can be useful as you become more and more familiar with the energetic body and sensitive to where you experience your blockages or obstacles.

THE OUTER *TSA LUNG* MOVEMENTS: THE BRIEF INSTRUCTIONS

The *tsa lung* movements work with breath retention, movement, and awareness to clear physical, emotional, and conceptual blockages and obstacles so that the practitioner can more easily recognize and abide in open awareness.

1.   Assume an upright seated posture.

2.   Bring your focus to the particular chakra being worked with.

3.   Connect with the stillness of your body, the silence of your inner speech, and the spaciousness of your mind.

4.   Bring to mind a challenge you currently face in your life. Draw attention inward and notice any tension in your body or any energetic disturbances. Become aware of thinking. Simply allow this experience without judging or analyzing. In this way you select.

5.   Inhale, reinhale, and focus breath, *lung*, and mind at the appropriate chakra while performing the *tsa lung* movements connected with that chakra. Release the breath through the chakra at the end of the movement. In this way you delete what has been selected. Inhalation and exhalation are done through the nose.

6.   Rest the mind in the open, clear space that becomes available in the chakra. In this way you become more familiar with openness as the source of positive qualities.

Upward-Moving *Lung*: Throat and Crown

Inhale and hold the breath, focusing at the throat. Reinhale.

Rotate the head five times counterclockwise, then five times clockwise.

Exhale, feeling the *lung* move up the throat chakra through the central channel and out through the crown chakra, dissolving into space.

Life-Force *Lung*: Heart

Inhale and hold the breath, focusing at the heart. Reinhale.

Make a lasso motion with the right arm, then the left arm.

Rotate the chest in a circular motion to the right, then to the left.

Exhale, feeling the *lung* from the heart chakra dissolving into space.

Fire-like *Lung*: Navel

Inhale and hold the breath at the navel with the vase hold: pull up the perineum and pelvic platform; press down with the diaphragm. Reinhale.

Rotate the navel area five times counterclockwise, then five times clockwise.

Exhale, feeling the *lung* from the navel chakra dissolving into space.

Pervasive *Lung*: Junction of the Three Channels

Inhale and hold the breath pervasively, throughout the whole body. Reinhale.

Clap your hands above your head, and rub them together, then massage the body; pull back on the bow to the right five times, then to the left five times.

Exhale, feeling the *lung* releasing through every pore of the body and dissolving into space.

Downward-Clearing *Lung*: Secret Chakra

Cross the right leg in front of the left. Inhale and pull up the perineum and pelvic platform in the basket hold. Reinhale.

Turn to the right knee and hold the knee; rotate five times counterclockwise.

Turn to the left knee and hold the knee; rotate five times clockwise.

Come to the center and hold both knees; rotate five times counterclockwise. Keep the focus on the spreading of *lung* in the secret chakra.

Exhale, feeling the *lung* release downward through the secret chakra, dissolving into space.

INSTRUCTIONS FOR THE INNER *TSA LUNG* EXERCISES

In addition to the five outer exercises, there are five inner *tsa lung* exercises. The inner *tsa lung* involves bringing the breath and the focus together to a particular chakra location and then retaining and releasing the breath. In some cases a supporting movement or a hold is employed. You can use reinhalation in each exercise, or you can perform them with a single inhalation. It is recommended that you repeat each exercise three times, and then rest in open awareness with your attention placed at the chakra while the experience remains fresh and uncontrived. Then shift your focus to the next chakra location and begin the exercise.

Upward-Moving Inner *Tsa Lung*

Inhale fresh, pure air while focusing at the throat chakra. Lightly pinch your nostrils together with the thumb and index finger of one hand. Hold your breath, applying a slight amount of pressure while imagining the *lung* expanding within your throat and rising upward through your head, cleansing the throat chakra and awakening the senses. Release your hold on the nostrils as you expel your breath through them, giving a final push with your diaphragm at the end of the exhalation. Imagine that the subtle *lung* shoots through the crown of your head and all your obscurations dissolve into space. Feel the opening at the throat and crown chakras and rest in open awareness. This exercise opens the central channel and increases clarity.

Life-Force Inner *Tsa Lung*

Inhale fresh, pure air, holding your breath while focusing at your heart chakra. Feel the *lung* expanding within your heart chakra, nourishing and cleansing this area. As you slowly release your breath through your nostrils, feel your heart releasing blockages and obscurations. Bring clear attention to whatever release or opening you feel in your heart, and rest in the openness and expansiveness you experience there. This exercise supports centered awareness and connection to positive qualities.

Fire-like Inner *Tsa Lung*

Inhale fresh, pure air while focusing at the navel chakra. Gently pull the navel toward the spine and hold your breath while maintaining this position. While holding your breath, imagine the *lung* warming and spreading within the navel chakra. Slowly release the breath and the hold, exhaling through the nose while imagining that the *lung* in the navel chakra releases, clearing any blockages and obscurations present there. Bring clear attention to the sense of openness at the navel and rest your attention there. This exercise promotes the experience of inner heat and the maturing of positive qualities.

Pervasive Inner *Tsa Lung*

Before doing this exercise, make sure the space behind you is clear and free of obstacles. Begin this exercise by sitting upright and exhaling completely while contracting your body in on itself: your hands and fingers curl inward, your arms are drawn in close to your chest, your knees come up, your spine curls over, and your head lowers toward your chest. Contract even the muscles of your face. Hold this contraction for a moment, and then slowly unfurl your body as you begin inhaling a fresh breath. Feel the pure air filling your entire body and extending through your limbs while you stretch your body expansively. At the peak of the inhalation and expansion, release your breath and fall gently backward, letting go completely onto the floor behind you as you fully exhale. Remain relaxed, resting in open awareness. This exercise supports the experience of the *lung* permeating through your body and beyond the bounds of your body. It supports the expression of spontaneous beneficial action in your life.

Downward-Clearing Inner *Tsa Lung*

Inhale fresh, pure air and bring your focus to the secret chakra. Hold the breath while pulling up on the muscles of the pelvic platform, the perineum, and the anus (basket hold). As you hold your breath and maintain the basket hold, imagine the *lung* cleansing and nurturing the secret chakra. Then slowly release the breath and the hold, breathing out through the nose while feeling the *lung* of the secret chakra releasing in a downward direction. Bring your attention to the secret chakra and rest there with open awareness. This exercise supports the experience of inner comfort and promotes fearless joyful action.

Instructions for the Secret *Tsa Lung* Exercises

There is a third set of *tsa lung* exercises, referred to as the secret *tsa lung*. In each of these exercises, a simple visualization supports the movement of light of a particular color in a specific chakra. As you hold your attention on the subtle movement of the colored light, the positive qualities of each chakra become more available. The light supports the practitioner's connection with the subtle *lung* that enables the recognition of the natural mind.

Upward-Moving Secret T*sa Lung*

Bring your attention to the throat chakra and imagine the upward movement of subtle *lung* in the form of yellow light rising up the central channel from the throat to the crown. At the crown, the *lung* spreads like the spokes of an open parasol, curving gently downward, nourishing the crown of your head. Rest your attention upon this subtle flow of yellow light.

Life-Force Secret *Tsa Lung*

At your heart chakra, imagine a clear, faceted crystal radiating white light in all directions, and rest your attention on this expanding white light.

Fire-like Secret *Tsa Lung*

At your navel chakra, imagine the subtle *lung* in the form of a wheel of red light slowly rotating counterclockwise. Rest your attention on the movement and the radiating red light.

Pervasive Secret *Tsa Lung*

At the junction of the three channels, four finger-widths below the navel, imagine green rays of light radiating in all directions throughout your body and beyond the bounds of your body. Rest your attention on this radiating green light.

Downward-Clearing Secret *Tsa Lung*

At the secret chakra, imagine blue light moving in a downward direction following the shape of downward-pointing bellows. Rest your attention in the flow of this blue light.

INFORMAL PRACTICE: APPLYING THE PRACTICE IN DAILY LIFE

Aside from the efficacy of bringing daily life challenges to your meditation, as we have been exploring, I also recommend that you bring your meditation to circumstances in your life as they are happening. Remember the refuge of stillness, silence, and spaciousness. In the middle of rushing around, stop and experience stillness; connect with your body directly. Be. In the middle of dinner at a restaurant, stop and listen to the silence. Sometimes taking a long inhalation, holding it, and releasing that breath up through the central channel and out the crown of your head can help you to shift your focus from feeling a complete lack of space to connecting with spaciousness.

For example, it is Saturday morning, and you have to go to the post office. You come through the door and see a long backed-up line. Everyone is carrying boxes. You mutter to yourself, "That clerk is being a little too talkative with each customer, as if the rest of us were not waiting in line with many more things on our to-do lists!" This is a familiar setup in which we may become increasingly annoyed, restless, and tense.

We all have our equivalent of this irritation. The question is, do we recognize it for what it is and shift it? We live far too much of our lives as if we were waiting for something outside of ourselves to change or to happen. That is the scary thing. We become victims of the circumstances of our lives. Secretly we feel,

"My life was not supposed to be this way." "I'm waiting for this person that I am living with to change." It's really quite sad. The tension in people's faces is readily observed as you look around. Many people look as if they are not in the right space. It is so important to recognize this in oneself and shift it.

Back at the post office, I can be miserable standing in line, or I can have a twenty-minute meditation of tension-free awareness. Either way, I am going to spend twenty minutes in that line. Do I recognize that I have a choice here? This is the perfect setup for the modern meditator and the perfect situation in which to become aware and to create a different space in oneself by using the power of attention. Our focus has power. Our experience is a result of our focus. When you feel bad, you can pretend to feel okay, but you are not okay. But even *before* you feel bad, the kind of focus you hold is leading you in the direction of misery, and it is important to become aware of that focus. We can change our focus, and that changes our experience.

Standing in line, I can shift my external focus to an internal one. I become aware of my preoccupation with my complaints about the talkative postal clerk and my long to-do list, and simply drop it. I shift my focus and feel my body, energy, and mind directly and nakedly. I inhale and bring my focus to the junction of the three channels and slowly release my breath up the central channel and through my crown, feeling that I am clearing the central channel. I do this three times and I feel more relaxed in my body, more peaceful in my energy, clearer in my mind. Now I draw my attention to my heart and connect there. Connecting there, I begin to notice some warmth. I am standing in a completely different space now. In that spaciousness there is so much more that is available and possible than I previously recognized. And I am certainly no longer a victim of my circumstances.

An even simpler practice in any challenging life situation is to bring your focus to your heart and perform the inner life-force *tsa lung* exercise: connect directly with any irritation or discomfort you are experiencing within your body, emotions, or mind; inhale and hold your breath while focusing at your heart; as you hold, imagine the warmth of the *lung* spreading in your heart, nourishing and cleansing this area. Release your breath slowly through your nostrils while also feeling that your heart is releasing tension and irritation and is becoming purified of any negativity. Do this a few times. Finally, simply rest in the spaciousness of your heart with open awareness, feeling the warmth of connecting with your open heart and feeling that warmth spreading throughout your body, radiating from your heart into the environment surrounding you.

CHAPTER THREE

THE NINE *LUNG*—A MAP OF TRANSFORMATION

As you continue to practice the Nine Breathings of Purification and the Five *Tsa Lung* Exercises, you will be able to more quickly and easily recognize your habitual patterns and, by using focus, breath, and movement, catch the winds that obscure openness and clear them through the three channels and the five chakras. As you recognize and become more familiar with the fundamental openness of your natural mind, you will discover a deep treasury within yourself.

There is more detail available about the nature of wind. The wind element can be described along a continuum from gross to subtle. It is possible to become more precise about the winds we are beginning to connect with and clear so that they no longer rule our lives and bring unfortunate consequences. For instance, when the grosser winds of our afflicting emotions and thoughts are cleared, a more subtle internal wind supports us to recognize our true nature, and in so doing we can enjoy the fruits of virtue that spontaneously arise from this natural mind. To continue exploring the path of transformation from confusion to wisdom, we can look at a description of nine *lung,* or winds, that describe a map of transformation.

KNOWING WHEN TO MAKE CHANGES IN LIFE

When we talk about transformation, we first need to consider the importance of recognizing the appropriate time in which to effect change. Very often people realize the need for change only after a disaster. For example, many become interested in world peace after engaging in a prolonged war. First we create and participate in war, and then, after massive destruction and loss of life, we become interested in world peace. On an individual level, perhaps only after you have almost destroyed your health do you then become motivated to make some changes. Although the resulting sense of waking up is certainly to be celebrated, sometimes that awakening comes rather late. The later it comes, the harder it is to make changes. This is something we are clearly aware of, and something that is simple common sense: the later it gets, the harder it is because it requires so much force, so much energy, and so much attention to make a change that we may come to a point where we don't have the energy required, let alone the skills to deal with making such a radical change. Sometimes we see the problem right in front of us and are unable to deal with it. We keep slipping into our addictions and habitual patterns. So *when* we intervene in the progression or development of a problem makes an enormous difference to the outcome. If we become aware of the development of an obscuration and intervene as early in the process as possible, we are able to clear the conflict before it gains momentum.

HAVING A SENSE OF WIND AND MIND

There are different approaches to making changes in the West, and at times some approaches touch on the territory of wind when speaking of the observer or when talking of waves and particles and energy. There is much depth and detail in the Eastern teachings, which speak about wind, or *lung*, in relation to liberation, becoming free of the suffering of existence altogether. If the Eastern teachings describe a path to liberation, then making a small life change in one human being should be very simple, right? If the ultimate change is to achieve liberation from suffering, changing your bad mood should not be a big deal. But failing to understand the wind and the mind makes it difficult to truly change, because the method used is often part of the problem itself.

What is meant by liberation from suffering? Recognizing the nature of mind, one is free from duality. When one's recognition is strong, duality does not affect one's essence. The meditator who is aware of the subtle winds is able to reverse duality, to catch or imprison the conceptual enemy and release it into the sky of nonconceptual awareness.

What is meant by reversing duality? Let's say one negative thought comes or one judgment arises in you. When you are able to recognize this and capture this wind and release it, that dualistic judging mind is not able to affect you. But when things degrade in life, it is because the conceptual mind arises and takes over. Emotions arise and take over. Needs and addictions arise and take over. When we clear this movement of wind through a practice such as the Nine Breathings, we are able to experience a more subtle awareness, awareness that recognizes the nature of mind rather than identifying with the moving mind. Through a practice such as the Nine Breathings, we are able to capture the wind of the dualistic, conceptual mind that travels between an apparently solid subject and an apparently solid object. The ability to overcome duality comes down to recognizing the structure of duality, the winds of our moving thoughts and afflicting emotions. As we capture and release various winds, we are able to overcome sickness and the imbalance of the elements, and maintain health. Through this process, the practitioner is able to recognize his or her basic nature. This recognition is not a product of the conceptual mind.

In the West, we talk about how we perceive, how we relate to things, how we understand things. The mind plays a big role in the psychology of transformation. The conceptual mind in particular has played a very important role, the nonconceptual mind has played a lesser role, and the wind has played no role. However, I think there can be no real sense of transformation unless there is knowledge of and experience of wind, and certainly there can be no transformation unless one experiences nonconceptual awareness. Conceptual awareness is important whenever that piece is needed in a particular situation. But that particular piece is not always needed. If you are aware at an earlier stage in the development of a problem, conceptual awareness is not needed at all. If you are aware at a later stage, the conceptual mind is useful. If you become aware too late, even the conceptual mind cannot play much of a role. "Too late" means that destruction is inevitable. If we are talking about a life, it is finished, and we die. If we are talking about a relationship, it ends. If we are talking about an environment, it is destroyed. It comes to the place where there is no way to reverse or change the outcome, because it is just too late to intervene with the result of previously unrecognized conditions.

Change is much easier to effect if you are willing to sit down and work with your breath. In our modern society, sitting down is not that easy. To sit down for even five minutes and work with the breath is not that common. There are some people who react to the suggestion to meditate in the same way a child reacts to being given a time-out. My little son goes to day care, and when he comes home, he gives my wife and me time-outs. You don't have to approach meditation as if it were a punishment.

Through connecting with your breath, you are able to rest much more deeply. You can discover deeper places in yourself, and then it becomes a matter of the length of time you rest in those deeper places. Through the breath, you are able to take a much deeper journey when you meditate. Your perspective—your view, your feelings, your experiences of positive qualities such as love— changes depending upon the way you rest in that inner space. We are becoming increasingly familiar with the scientific idea of the observer changing reality. According to these Eastern teachings, there is no question about it: the observer will change the reality. In ordinary life we know so many situations where the observer does change the reality. But it is important to question what we mean by "observer." Are we talking about the observer who has totally messed up, the observer who is about to mess up, the observer who is thinking about messing up, or the observer who has the potential to mess up? All of those are observers. And we can be any one of those observers at different times and in different situations in life. So which observer is it we are talking about?

THE NOTION OF BODY

When we engage in the practice of meditation, we can develop an increasingly subtle sense of observation. In Bön Buddhism, these different stages of observation are referred to as "bodies." There is a description of nine stages of *lung* that I'd like to introduce as a tool or map of transformation. This map describes each of these stages of observation, each of which is actually a kind of body. And that body can either support creative, positive energies or act out destructive energies. The highest body attainable is the changeless essence body. This is the body of the eternal now, of pure presence, and it corresponds to the first level of *lung*, called the *lung* of the space of *bön* nature. A grosser body is the changeable karmic conceptual pain body.

Ignorance, the root of all suffering, is basically the failure to recognize that essential space, that changeless body referred to in the first level of *lung*. Through ignorance we have lost contact with that space, lost the connection, lost the awareness, lost the trust in, even lost the sense of direction toward that essential space. All this loss is the outcome of ignorance. When one does not know oneself, there is ignorance. When there is ignorance, there is the vision of ignorance, which means that our experiences and appearances arise from the lack of recognition. The perceiver arises from ignorance. That perceiver is the product of ignorance. And what you, the perceiver, perceive, since you do not recognize that what you are seeing is yourself, is something other, something "out there." Thus duality is created. When you see something other, the only way to go is "I like it," or "I don't like it." I like it—attachment. I don't like it—aversion, anger. The words *attachment* and *anger* may sound extreme, but our tendency is to either hold on to an experience or push it away. There is no neutral experience. We have yes or no. Even in a general way in life, whenever we have a more neutral or accepting relationship to our experiences, we feel much better. It is more peaceful to not constantly engage in a yes/no or good/bad evaluation of our experiences. There is a more neutral place from which to experience life, a place of breathing, seeing, and experiencing the world in a much easier and more open way. So we shift from the reaction of yes or no to the sense of observer, and that observer can become increasingly subtle until it merges altogether into the clear and open space of the unchanging body.

Most of the time we experience a changeable body, the karmic conceptual pain body. A common experience of this changeable body occurs when we feel low in self-confidence. "I'm not good enough," we tell ourselves. Perhaps there is a place in your life where these feelings come into play. Take a moment now and think of a situation of challenge in your life. As you do this, you may notice some discomfort in your body. It's as if the part of you experiencing this difficult situation is another being with its own sense of body, even to the point of altering your posture. You can discover a shift in the energetic dynamic in your body; perhaps anxiety or certain emotions come into play. If you listen to your inner dialogue, you may discern a certain view or logic at work as you compare yourself unfavorably with others or indulge in self-criticism. Whether we perceive the changeable body physically, emotionally, or conceptually, experiencing life in this way becomes so familiar that we may become resigned to a stressful existence.

Sometimes we get very stuck there, and our whole existence becomes based on that pain. We love from that pain. We connect from that pain. We hate because of that pain. We do things in life because of that pain, or we stop doing things because of that pain. And that pain becomes our total operating system. You need to recognize: Who is the one who is afraid? Who is the one who doubts? Who is that? That identity is not who you really are. It is not your authentic being. It is a habit, a structure of wind that can be released, freeing your consciousness to become more subtly present and alive and vital.

As important as it is to recognize this, it is much more important not to analyze or judge this experience; simply feel it. Spend a moment of stillness with whatever you are feeling. Spend a moment of silence with whatever you are feeling. Connect with spaciousness and release the tendency to judge or analyze your experience. Simply be with what you experience directly.

The Nine *Lung* and Their Resulting Actions

The list of the nine *lung* describes patterns of wind and shows the possibility of breaking certain patterns either in your individual life or in a broader group or collective life pattern. So in you as an individual, in family life, in society at large, or in the world, there are patterns that can be discerned and changed. We need to bring these teachings down to earth, because that is where we are.

The wisdom teachings describe a path to complete enlightenment. Not everyone is interested in achieving enlightenment yet, but most of us want to have some goodness in life. And that is sufficient reason to reflect a little closer on wind and mind and on what these teachings have to offer.

Here is a simplified list of the nine *lung,* or winds, and their resulting actions from subtle to gross:

1. The *lung* of the space of *bön* nature: abides in essential nature

2. The *lung* of the bliss of primordial wisdom: awakens wisdom

3. The *lung* of self-arising innate awareness: spontaneously rests in the nature of mind

4. The *lung* of the horse of the mind: causes movement of thoughts

5. The *lung* of the force of karma: determines the direction of any transition

6. The *lung* of the coarse mental afflictions: causes expression of the negative emotions (the five poisons: anger, greed, ignorance, jealousy, and pride)

7. The *lung* that disturbs the humors of the body: causes disease through the imbalance of negative emotions

8. The *lung* of the power of existence: constructs beings and their environments

9. Era-destroying *lung*: causes actions of destroying beings and their environments

In order to explore the presence of these winds in our life, let us begin with the grossest wind first and move progressively to the more subtle winds, since the grosser winds are more obvious.

9. Era-Destroying *Lung*

As its name implies, the era-destroying wind is destructive. It can refer to collective forces such as the collective fears that lead to the decision to go to war and the resulting devastation of life and landscape. It can refer to the forces of materialism and their effect upon the global environment, with the resulting destruction of ecosystems and the earth's atmosphere. Or it can refer to cutting off or terminating a relationship, or ending one's perceived pain through a violent act such as suicide.

8. The *Lung* of the Power of Existence

The *lung* of the power of existence on an individual level can refer to an extreme sense of overidentification with one's profession or status in life, which results in not having much flexibility to change. If you identify yourself as a victim of circumstance, it is difficult to even perceive opportunities for change. On the collective level, societies rally around belief systems, campaign slogans, and convictions that reinforce an illusion of being the way things are.

Most of us find our everyday experiences in the areas of numbers 7 through 4 on the chart of the nine *lung*. So this is where we will focus more of our exploration.

7. The *Lung* That Disturbs the Humors of the Body

The *lung* that disturbs the humors of the body leads to sickness and disease. Perhaps you have some kind of sickness or pain in your body, or you fear that some illness is there. To explore this further, begin by connecting with stillness, silence, and spaciousness. From that open place, look directly at your experience of pain or illness. Let your mind travel through your body to a particular area. Sometimes you may clearly know that your sickness has to do with your anger, attachment, or ignorance. According to Tibetan medicine, every disease is connected with these three root poisons. But how can you precisely know this? At the very least you can have some sense of that association, which is sufficient to work with in meditation.

As you bring your attention to the sense of pain or disease, connect with the experience directly and do the Nine Breathings.

If you have the time, breathe nine times for each of the three channels for a total of twenty-seven breaths. Each time you breathe out, make a conscious bridge from those areas of illness in the body to the channels as you release the tensions in that area of the body, and direct the breath through the channels as you exhale.

Once you have done the actual physical part of the breathing exercise, go back into the same place, bringing a feeling of openness. With openness, look at that area of the body; journey into the body again. Take a moment to think about someone who you feel is your best friend. What are the qualities of that best friend that make you feel relaxed, make you feel you can be who you are, make you feel you can say stupid or silly things? You don't need to pretend to be anybody with this person; you just relax. So because that friend has some real sense of openness toward you and doesn't judge you, how do you feel? You feel great. In the same way, think that after the exercise, you are your own best friend. You are the best friend of the one who is sick. You are the best friend of the one who is going through pain. At that moment, look with open attention, even if only for five minutes. Looking in that area in this way *is* the healing.

It is important to continue and repeat this practice until you become very, very familiar with that place of open awareness. Normally we do not do that. Instead we engage in negative self-talk: "What's wrong with me?" When you look at that part of your body, you say: "I am sick. This is the area of my sickness. This is the area of my pain. This is the area of my problem. This is the one who is going to take me over." There is somebody who is giving all those fearful messages to that area of the body. But now, the one who is looking is no longer that judging person. It's a totally different person. It's a friend. As I said, have the image of a best friend to support the principle of open awareness. Of course, in order to have some degree of openness, we do the Nine Breathings. We may need to do more than three breaths for each channel in order to clear our tendencies to push our experience away, grasp or fill in the moment, or disconnect entirely in order to come to this place of feeling enough openness to simply be with our experience.

So we are saying that breathing out the three poisons of aversion/anger, attachment/greed, and ignorance has everything to do with your sickness. There is a wind that causes disease. And that wind has a characteristic of the three poisons. Poison makes you sick. So you are associating your experience of the three poisons with your disease. As a result of breathing out, you feel some degree of openness and especially openness in relation to your tensions, pains, and sickness, relaxing the sense of being sick and releasing your identity as one who is sick. You are allowing the better individual to emerge—the authentic person in yourself. You allow that person to look. That person brings totally different information and energy to the place of sickness. And then it is a matter of ten or fifteen minutes, to half an hour, to one hour, as you establish a regular pattern of five times a day to ten times a day until it becomes a pattern that pervades your life. If that becomes a pattern in your life, there is a much greater chance to heal your sickness.

6. The *Lung* of the Coarse Mental Afflictions

We have been trying to recognize the frequency of certain emotional states in our lives and to recognize that something is influencing our emotions. For example, take number 6, the *lung* of coarse mental afflictions. This refers to the five negative emotions of anger, greed, ignorance, jealousy, and pride. They are common to all schools of Buddhism and are known as the five poisons. Among these five poisons we have already begun to explore the three root poisons—anger, attachment, and ignorance. Every experience of suffering can find its root cause within these three poisons. It is possible to examine your own life and find these three poisons. You can know where they manifest, you can know how it feels to experience them, and you can also reflect upon your ability or inability to handle them properly.

While you may know that these coarse mental afflictions, or negative emotions, exist in you and influence your life, you may not be aware of what causes them to do so. What kind of energy is causing your anger? You may have never paid close attention to this. In many of the practices that I have been teaching in recent years, I encourage my students to look at a difficult situation, connect with the emotion that arises as they do so, and discover the presence of that emotion in the body, breath, and mind. That is a core approach. The reason we bring the experience of the emotion back into the body, breath, and mind is to understand the energetic structure of our discomfort and suffering rather than the conceptual story line. As a state of mind, anger is difficult to control. We tend to justify and rationalize our anger, but this only fortifies it. But if you become aware of the energy that anger rides, you can work directly with that energy and shift it. That will then influence the mind of anger. So whether it's anger or any of the negative emotions, the idea is to focus on the energy of the emotion itself rather than on the story line. "Focus on the energy" is another way of saying "connect with the wind." This is the meaning behind the analogy of catching the horse (energy) and then guiding it in a positive direction along the path (channels of the body) to liberation (openness).

The first suggestion for catching the horse is to see where the horse appears. Look at the situation, the place where you get angry, or bring to mind the person you're angry at. It is easiest if you recognize your own anger in the moment when you are feeling it.

But you can also work with a recollection of anger, remembering when you felt it in the past. Just acknowledging that you get angry, recognizing those moments and experiences, and feeling those experiences is the way to catch that horse. You can reflect on it by saying: "Last week I was really angry at that person." You recognize your emotion: "I felt angry." Just bringing it to mind, you can feel the agitation in your body, and the disturbance in your breath. This is not about judging yourself or another person, or weighing the merits of getting angry or not. Here you are just trying to remember, trying to acknowledge that you did get angry. You remember in such a way that the experience becomes fresh in this moment, and you feel it. Whatever the experience of anger is in this moment, or whatever experience the recollection of anger brings, you feel it. The moment you feel it in your body and feel how it affects your breath, there is a good chance that you're connecting with that particular wind called the *lung* of the coarse mental afflictions. It is very likely that you are catching or have caught that horse.

The point is not to analyze or judge the anger, but to feel the wind that supports that anger, the wind that influences that anger, the wind that gives rise to that anger. Connect with that wind. The only way to really do it—I'll repeat this again—is by bringing the attention back to your body and awakening that experience of anger in your body and in your breath. Then you are catching the horse. Catching the horse, meaning the wind, is easier than catching the rider, the mind. Guiding the horse is the easiest way to guide the rider. So this is a particular approach to dealing with negative situations.

Once we begin to feel some sense of the effect of doing the Nine Breathings practice, with respect to the coarse mental afflictions, the negative emotions, and the three root poisons, seeing change means you are clearing something deeper than the story line.

5. The *Lung* of the Force of Karma

It is important to recognize anger *directly*. If you ask why you get angry, your conceptual mind has some answers: "That person is mean and has repeatedly and intentionally done hurtful things, and has intentionally done hurtful things to me. *He* is the one with the anger problem." You have wonderful reasons to justify your anger, right? These are the answers that come when you ask why you get angry. Now, if you ask the question "Is this anger really necessary?" another kind of answer arises. You say: "Well, from the practice point of view, maybe anger is not so necessary. These are all illusions; I don't have to engage with them." You may think that, but the question still remains: why do you continue to get angry? And that's a good question. You get angry because there is a strong wind, and with it comes some sense of hopelessness or powerlessness. You don't have the power or strength to stop it. You don't have the wisdom to stop it. You are not awake in those moments when anger arises. That could be referred to as "the wind of the force of karma" blowing. The force of karma has the effect that sometimes you don't know where you are or how you ended up at the place where you find yourself. You say: "How did I get in this situation?" It is as if you were asking somebody else. After all the actions you took, after everything you wanted, when you start to suffer as a result, you then ask: "How come I am here?" It seems like that is not a very good question. The reason you're asking that question may be that whatever you are experiencing is not what you wanted to experience. "It's not really what I intended. I don't know how I got here."

Clearly there are winds apart from your will, winds that push you in directions you didn't intend to go. Those winds exist in us. In Bön teachings, those winds are acknowledged. When we do a purification practice, we are not doing it because we have messed up our life. We are doing purification practice because we *might* mess up our life. We are purifying the potential, or "burning the seeds." We are burning the seeds so that they don't grow and ripen into negative fruits. Burning the seeds is important, and we can burn karmic seeds by recognizing the roots.

In working with number 6, the *lung* of the coarse mental afflictions, we are trying to recognize the seeds and roots of our negative emotions. In a karmic situation, it is not so easy to know. You can't say, "My karma is exactly there." It won't be like that. But clearly, the wind of the force of karma might be there, and the more you are able to clear your emotional wind, the more you can come to a place of clarity and see that there is something you have no power over. It just drives you to do certain things. Seeing and openly recognizing this helps. Open recognition means recognizing something without judgment.

How do we work with number 5, the *lung* of the force of karma? You want to have awareness. The awareness is very simply recognizing that there is some force beyond rationality that pushes you in a certain direction. You are trying to be aware of and connect with that force, or wind. You try to clear that wind through the Nine Breathings exercise. The force of karma is basically a wind, or *lung,* that pushes you in a certain direction without your choice, without your will. Sometimes you think that's what you want; sometimes you know that it's not what you want. But still it doesn't change its direction. Until the wind of the force of karma is cleared, it pushes you in a certain direction. Of course, the force of karma is not necessarily bad—that is important to understand. When we purify, we purify the negative karmic winds. Sometimes we cultivate the positive karmic winds. I think many healing rituals are ways of cultivating positive karmic winds.

I encourage you to consistently recognize the three root poisons and how they appear in number 6, the *lung* of the coarse mental afflictions, and in number 5, the *lung* of the force of karma; and also what they mean in number 4, the *lung* of the horse of the mind. While our awareness may shift to noticing different aspects of our experience, the method we apply is the same: the Nine Breathings of Purification. When we are seeking to clear the wind of the force of karma, we are less personally engaged with the three root poisons. There is more recognition of how they arise in us when we are working with number 5. There is a sense of more openness than when we are working with the wind of the coarse mental afflictions, or the negative emotions.

So our inner work is to remember these three root poisons. Even though there are five negative emotions, remember that there are three root poisons. The method is always the Nine Breathings of Purification. Through the Nine Breathings we develop different awareness, different understanding. The tool is the same. We are trying to recognize the three root poisons; we just stay with that. With the *lung* of the coarse mental afflictions, we are trying to relate to the horse, or the energy, of the emotion itself, rather than engaging with the rider, or the story line. And then, once you can feel the relation with the horse, use the tool. Once you feel the connection to the horse, the Nine Breathings is a very powerful practice. It has power, but without connecting clearly with one's life, it is just breathing. So if you are able to release the winds of the coarse mental afflictions, the negative emotions, then your chances of working with the karmic winds are better.

So with the karmic winds, just be aware of certain forces that are in you, forces that move you in a certain direction; then create a positive intention: "Through the Nine Breathings, may I clear those winds." It could be a simple intention like that. There is some sense of awareness that there is a force. It is not just the anger itself, but being able to feel the force, the power of this force that drives you in that direction. If you pay attention to it, sometimes you can feel it. "I didn't want to get angry, but I almost felt pushed in that direction." So when you find yourself noticing or saying something like that, in that moment just close your eyes and feel it. What you just said—feel it. The moment you express that, close your eyes and just be openly aware of what you just said. There is a chance that you are connecting with that karmic wind because that wind is active in that moment. But if you are thinking, you are not going to connect; thinking does not connect. So the moment you are aware of it and say, "I don't know. It really pushes me," in that very moment just close your eyes and feel that. You are selecting it. I always say: "Select properly." That is the only way you can delete it or release it or guide it. If you don't select it properly, pressing the delete button doesn't help. Selecting means to be aware without judgment, and to feel it in your body and breath. That is the way of selecting. How far we can go is a more complicated issue. But this is what we need to try.

The way to connect with the karmic wind is to recognize the force that is beyond your will. Tibetan people often say, "Oh, it's my karma." You may also hear people in the West use that expression: "It's my karma." What does that mean—"It's my karma"? Does that mean that you don't have a choice? "It's my karma. I have to accept it." "It's my karma. I don't know what to do." "It's my karma. Maybe nothing can be done." You can hear a sense of hopelessness and powerlessness being expressed. Karmic forces are beyond your will or intention. There is some sense of that. So when the karmic wind blows, you cannot really change what is happening, but you can change the causes that will make it happen the next time. The basic point is to be aware that there is something beyond your will. There are forces that are beyond the reach of the will. Karma is such a force. It is important to understand that there is karma. It is important to believe in the existence of karma until you fully realize it. If there is no sense of trust or willingness to understand the existence of karma, you are not going to release your karma, and you are more likely to continue acting in ways that perpetuate karma. Basically, acknowledging the existence of karma is acknowledging the possibility of transformation. Because at some point, transformation is not just about what skills or good ideas you have; there is something deeper than that. If you are aware of that and you work with it, perhaps you will be more hopeful in the face of a challenge.

4. The *Lung* of the Horse of the Mind

There is a subtle wind that produces thought. In our practice of meditation, after experiencing the dissolution of negative emotions and the dissolution of the force of karma, it is possible to feel a deep sense of opening. In this openness you can still feel very subtle movements of thoughts, even as you are very clear and open. Silly, stupid, funny, meaningless, or meaningful thoughts move but don't disturb your awareness. You do not even track or remember what the thoughts were. Nonetheless, there are still thoughts. So it is possible to be aware of the movement of thoughts, and yet in that awareness, none of your thoughts disturb you. Your thoughts are not interfering with being present. That means there is a very subtle wind that is still there. You can feel the movement of this subtle wind, and this movement tricks these thoughts to come. There is no particular reason for some of these thoughts, but for whatever reason, there are thoughts.

During those moments, bring your attention to observing the observer; look at the one who is feeling very open. This opens the space up a little bit more. There is a lot of openness already there, but another depth is possible. At some point in your meditation practice there is something that is not easily dissolved by using the exhalation, so observing the observer causes the deeper dissolution. Again, when we feel some deeper space, there can still be a subtle movement. We may feel so open, but there can still be the subtle movement of the observer. There is somebody smart who is realizing the truth. You have to release your identification with that smart being. What produces the observer, what holds that smart being, is a subtle wind. Here it is not so much about doing deep breathing or doing some exercise to release this wind; rather, it is the position of mind itself that brings the release. When you look directly at who is observing, that has the releasing power equal to the power of releasing through the breath in the earlier stages. This pattern of wind shifts when the observer observes the one who is observing.

According to the dzogchen teachings, first the object is dissolved; then it is suggested to observe the observer. The outcome is that both the observed and the observer dissolve. Why do you want to dissolve anything? Because you want to connect to the essential space of open awareness. The lack of the dissolution of forms, which are the products of duality, is the obstacle to directly connecting with that essential space, which is why we are interested in dissolving all these layers. That is why the inner refuge is stillness, silence, and spaciousness.

Perhaps the space of your meditation practice is much clearer than before, and perhaps that space is the space you are not too familiar with. When that experience becomes more familiar, that space allows wisdom to occur. Wisdom is the recognition of the eternal body. If you think about progressively dissolving the obstacles as we have been discussing, you come to experience number

3, the *lung* of self-arising, innate awareness, just being aware, being aware of something, being aware again of something, and then being aware that "I am aware of that awareness."

And so at the end of the releasing breaths of the Nine Breathings of Purification, the instruction is to totally rest in that openness—in that stillness, in that silence, in that spaciousness. If you pay very close attention internally, you feel this very subtle wave, movement, or motion. Look back at who is resting, at who is feeling this openness, at who is aware of this openness. Directly, nakedly, look inward, backward, and see who. The moment you look at who it is, both observer and observed dissipate. Rest in the inseparable state of observer and observed. Look again, dissolve, rest. Repeat this a few times until you clearly experience it.

Each of us will have different experiences in our meditation practice. The main emphasis is that by connecting with very concrete issues of anger, attachment, and ignorance in your life and by not going into the story of those issues, you can connect to the very structure of the emotions themselves. In the practice of the Nine Breathings of Purification, we are connecting to the wind and releasing that from the channels in the body. As a result, it is possible to gain a deeper connection to a sense of peace. As you repeat this same exercise, you can increasingly feel this peace. Is that true or not? Alternatively, you can dwell on the story about who you are angry at and why you are angry, and come to the conclusion: "Yes, I feel the same way toward that person. As long as they are acting that way I'm going to feel angry. I am maintaining the same position because it is the same situation. I feel I have the right to relate to that person in this way." You can form a club around your stance. But can you see the power and the effect of the practice to recognize and dissolve your stance altogether? Of course, you can think: "Well, I am feeling at peace *now*, but I haven't really changed." That may be true at first, but you certainly haven't changed by dwelling on your anger, either. Here you are in the position to make a change. You are moving in the direction of change, because as the winds are getting subtler and subtler, your experiences of yourself are getting deeper and deeper. And what arises from those experiences in the form of thoughts and emotions changes. As our thoughts and emotions come up, our relation to them is completely different. That is called change.

So how do you notice change? For me, change will be seeing if, as a result of doing this practice over time, I am beginning to have a completely different relation to the thoughts and feelings about the person at whom I have been so angry. As my relationship to my feelings and thoughts opens up, the very nature of my seemingly solid story line changes. There are simply more possibilities available in that flexible space of awareness. That is called change. If I am having the same patterns of thought, if I am feeling angry and thinking about it continuously, I cannot call that change. Perhaps I am having worse thoughts, meaning I come up with more reasons to stay angry and continuously validate my view of that person: "I have a right to get angry; I have every reason to get angry; it's good to get angry; I know it is my friend who needs to change." That is also change, but in the wrong direction.

When you release anger through the Nine Breathings of Purification, you experience the cessation of anger. You connect with the space of the absence of the anger. You are feeling stability in that space. You are feeling familiarity in that space. If that is true, a different wind is moving now. So the moment I am aware of that space, another, more subtle wind has moved in. Without any effort, I am aware of it; I am aware of that greater space in myself. The moment I am aware of it, I know the wind has changed.

Let's explore this question about the observer creating the reality. When the coarse mental afflictions are activated, this means we are experiencing strong negative emotions such as anger. Perhaps attachment is strong and you are disconnected from yourself. Your view of reality or place of observation is determined by the conflicting negative emotions that you are experiencing. You aren't very stable. This is not the best place from which to observe things. The reality that you are creating by observing from that place is not a good one. Every thought you have and the resulting decisions you are going to make are not good. You make a decision and you think that is the best decision you can make, but actually that is the only decision that you can make under such conditions. But if you keep on working with the practice, you can come to a place of feeling more openness. You can minimize the presence of the wind of the coarse mental afflictions, the negative emotions. It is the same with the wind of the force of karma. You can release this wind through practice. More open space is available. You experience the cessation of those winds. Then it is possible that your observations come from observing the space itself, and that space itself is the source of positive qualities. Familiarity with that space will give birth to amazing things. The cessation of anger can give birth to love, for example. When the grosser emotional wind of anger is released, there is some connection with the karmic wind of that anger that can now purify. When you find some cessation of that karmic wind, you abide there.

You might ask: "When I am not feeling angry anymore, why do I have to abide there?" That is a good question, and the answer is that you want to abide, or rest, there because you want to discover the positive qualities, such as love, that can emerge from that space. The soil is ready, but you want to receive the fruit. After you cut the weeds in a garden, you plant seeds. At that point you cannot say, "It's done." It is not done. That is not the time of harvest. What do you do? You observe the seeds; you observe how they are growing. You nourish the seeds. What do you give them? You give them water and light. The more moisture and light, the more growth occurs.

So at the moment of release or cessation, the moment you see the space, you are discovering the soil in which the positive quality grows. And the way the quality grows is through open awareness. Open awareness within the space that opens up when a negative emotion clears needs to be maintained consistently, just as water and heat need to be consistent. When soil is prepared by removing the weeds, and there is sufficient water and heat, over time plants grow and their fruit ripens. But if the water or the heat stops, even if the seeds are present they will not germinate. Even if the winds of the coarse mental afflictions and the force of karma are exhausted, if you don't maintain awareness of that space, it will not give birth. In the West we seem to have an appreciation for methods of clearing and exhausting negative emotions. But the second piece—attention to the space—is missing. The first piece, clearing, seems to be acknowledged. But acknowledging the cessation, acknowledging the space, is not. Most people would simply experience space by saying, "There is nothing there." What is meant by "There is nothing there"? It means there is no-*thing* there; there is no stuff there. We are used to stuff. Material things have meaning for us. If we don't accumulate stuff, there is no meaning in life. Stuff is the way we identify ourselves. Without stuff, we don't exist. So the moment of openness is not always appreciated for what it is and for the potential that it actually has, because we have already moved on to the next project, the next relationship, the next idea, which is all stuff. Because of our addiction to stuff, which includes thoughts and emotions, we are not fully able to cultivate the genuine internal positive qualities that are available. Maintaining open awareness in the space that has been cleared is the necessary missing piece.

So the point I am trying to make here—I always touch this issue in different ways—is to not doubt the space. You must trust the space. And what does that mean? That means if you dissolve things and achieve that space and rest in that space, you know that that space has value. That is the space that gives birth to everything. The experience of that space gives birth to the experience of love. It is the very space that births the ability to experience love. It is the space that creates a whole reality of love or a whole reality of peace, whether in your family or in society or in the whole world or in the entire universe. The ability to create that reality is the power of that space. But we have to trust that power. We have to know that that is how positive change evolves. Again, that is why there is an emphasis upon stillness, silence, and spaciousness as the inner refuge, as the place to turn when we are confused or lost. And the necessary foundation for refuge is trust.

By contrast, we clearly have so many experiences of striving and pushing that never work. We have many experiences of trying in the wrong area and never having a positive result. How long have you been trying to be happy? Trying to be happy is a waste of time. But trusting the space of being as the source of happiness does work. We are not just talking about space; we are talking about very, very specific things here. You are trying to understand your anger in very specific karmic situations in your life. "I am angry at my boss." In this practice, we are not interested in your detailed story about your boss. That's not what is of concern here. You are being encouraged to relate to anger in a very specific way. From an open place of stillness, silence, and a spacious mind, you are being encouraged to connect with that emotion directly, to allow the experience fully without pushing it away or producing all manner of stories or disconnecting from it. As you fully allow that emotion, you can clearly experience the energy below the story line. There is a wind; there is a horse, an energetic structure. It is clearly there and you can connect with it and shift it through the practice of the Nine Breathings of Purification. In so doing, you will shift your reality.

You cannot change your emotions by force, through an imposition of will. But by connecting with their underlying structure, the wind, or the horse, that the emotions ride, it is possible to release that structure and change your experience. When we bring our attention to the body and particularly to the breath, it is easy to notice how emotions affect our breathing. Sometimes you may catch yourself holding or restricting your breath in the presence of emotion. Or you may find that your breath becomes rapid and shallow. There is a relationship between your breath and the coarse mental afflictions.

When you are breathing out many times while directing your awareness through the white right channel, you are altering the structure of mental afflictions such as anger or pride or jealousy. The coarse wind is much weaker now. This is something you can feel. And when you draw attention to the channel, it feels much lighter. If you repeat the practice with the left channel, you can feel the shift there as well. As you repeat this process again with the central channel, you can feel the shift in the entire central part of your body. You can feel some space opening up within you. As you connect with that spaciousness, become familiar with it. Go deeper into it. The central channel is a path to the changeless space, and the only way to journey into that space is to have a subtle horse to ride. The untamed horses of the mental afflictions and the force of karma need to be released. As you discover the spaciousness and allow it, be with it without following or identifying with any thoughts that arise; you will find a more subtle horse, a more subtle wind.

When you connect with spaciousness, rest there. Be there. As you rest in the stillness, silence, and spaciousness, whatever amount of time you are able to remain changes you. This will change something in you, probably much more than the many other things you may do to work with your anger. You can have ten hours of conversation with your friend about your anger. You can spend a whole weekend exploring how and why you get angry with somebody. But I totally believe there is no comparison between ten hours of conversation and ten minutes of resting in the space of the cessation of the anger. With respect to which method will transform me, with respect to my relation to anger and the movement of anger into love or into higher experiences of wisdom, there is no comparison. Is this true for everybody? Perhaps not. Some people might consider a ten-hour conversation better because that's the only thing they are familiar with. It doesn't mean that's the best thing for them, it simply means it's the only way they know. If it is the best thing someone can do at the time, it has value. But it is not the best method possible.

Trusting the space that becomes available when anger clears is essential. It is that very space in which the quality of love will emerge. I often give the following example that one of my students shared with me. He was having a hard time with a colleague at work. They were having difficulties in their work relationship, and this student was working to clear those issues through his meditation practice. One morning he was ordering a coffee for himself and suddenly out of his mouth came: "Two coffees, please." This person found himself getting one coffee for himself and one for the colleague who used to be his difficult person. Somehow the thought to buy coffee for this person spontaneously and genuinely came. So that thought, that little kindness, will manifest without any schedule. And in this way you witness that your life is changing, and your life keeps on changing. The changes are not made by direct effort or an imposition of will. They come spontaneously because you clear the obstacles that block your positive qualities from emerging. That's all you do, and the changes just happen by themselves. These are changes we can trust. What we usually do is the opposite. Instead of clearing the path, we try to force the result. And then we fail. We are guaranteed to fail for the rest of our lives if we keep on doing that. There is no way we will change through forcing a result. But if we release the blockages that keep us from being open and then connect with and trust the openness, the result will naturally arise from there.

3. The *Lung* of Self-Arising Innate Awareness

The *lung* of self-arising innate awareness refers to the capacity of each individual to awaken and recognize the union of space and awareness. When I am not conscious, I lose the connection to openness and fall into ignorance. I experience doubt and insecurity. But when I am awake, I am awake in that union. In the tradition of dzogchen, your teacher introduces you to your natural mind, which is usually unrecognized. When we enter into the space of the union of openness and awareness, that space is the nature of mind. When we talk about meditating, that is what we are talking about. We know union is always there. When we enter into that space, we are connected to that. Meditation practice celebrates the capacity to recognize openness and to trust it. Not allowing our conceptual mind or ignorance to interfere with that union, we allow all thoughts, feelings, sensations, and memories to arise, dwell, and dissolve without struggle. We rest in that space of open awareness. That is how we continue—we abide in the recognition of the union of space and awareness. Practicing for half an hour, 45 minutes, or one hour, you continuously expand your ability to maintain connection to that recognition, such that eventually movements, sounds, and thoughts can never disturb your connection to that union, and instead they become an ornament of the union itself.

If you experience conscious innate awareness, you have the introduction to the nature of mind, and this affects your moving mind quite positively. You discover a lot of hidden qualities such as compassion, love, and joy. Having connection to that union is like discovering a hidden treasure. Think of this one image: You have the key to the treasury. The treasury is the union—the union of essence and wisdom, mother and son, space and light, openness and awareness. However this union is described, your key is your conscious awareness. So when you open the treasury with the key of your conscious awareness, you have everything that you need. I'm not talking about a brand-new car, but all the qualities we seek in our life, such as joy, hope, enthusiasm, trust, and confidence, are just there. When you open to the moment and connect with conscious awareness, the positive qualities emerge. Whatever is appropriate spontaneously arises in whatever circumstance you find yourself in.

If you are with people who are neither friends nor family but are just neutral to you, and if one of them experiences difficulty or pain, you naturally and spontaneously feel the effortless willingness to help that person, even though he is not someone you are close to. The spontaneous action of loving-kindness will arise in you because it is in you at the source, and you have a connection with the source. It will not come spontaneously if you have lost the connection, however. If you have lost the key to that inner treasure, if you have lost awareness, spontaneous love will not arise. What I'm talking of here is how our conscious recognition of number 3, the *lung* of self-arising innate awareness, affects number 4, the *lung* of the horse of the mind, which is the moving mind, our thoughts. The qualities will emerge. If they are not forthcoming in a situation, when you see that somebody is going through pain and it doesn't move your heart, that means your heart needs to be exercised in practice. You need to allow the disconnection and distractions to dissolve and the recognition to dawn. You need to connect with the space of your heart in a warmer and deeper and more profound way.

2. The *Lung* of the Bliss of Primordial Wisdom

The second wind has to do with awakening wisdom, which means *being aware* of essence, of the essential space of being. This awareness is supported by subtle wind, and traditionally, there are five wisdoms: the wisdom of emptiness, mirror-like wisdom, the wisdom of equanimity, discriminating wisdom, and all-accomplishing wisdom. How might we experience wisdom in our everyday life? There are times during which you can be very open and remain that way for an extended period. It is also possible that even when the experience of openness is available to you, you do not recognize it as such. The moment you recognize openness, it's very powerful. Just being aware of what you are feeling as you are feeling it is powerful. So often our relationship to our self and our communication with others is storied. We basically spend our time reporting on experiences that happened yesterday or might happen tomorrow, so that often we don't fully show up for what is actually happening in the moment. Here I am referring to the awareness of openness as wisdom. Openness is the state of the changeless essence body, which is the first wind; being aware of that changeless body is wisdom, the second wind.

1. The *Lung* of the Space of *Bön* Nature

The chart begins with the essential *lung* of the *bön* nature. What kind of wind is this? What state of reality is this referring to? This refers to our essential nature, meaning a sense of the essence of everything: the essence of form and the essence of consciousness; the essence of the environment, or container, and the essence of the contents. When you are in a deep meditation, when thoughts and emotions are not active, when you are simply breathing, you can arrive at the place where you are basically one with the universe. Many of us have glimpsed some experience of essence, have been touched or stirred by nature in such a way that we may feel we have glimpsed the sacred. Many of us have moments of experiencing this because this is what *is*. We feel so restful and yet so alive, at peace, and connected to all of life. In that sense of oneness we experience so much potentiality and aliveness. So there are moments when we experience that. For many people this could be similar to the experience of the *lung* of the space of *bön* nature, and for some people it could actually *be* the experience.

This is something that connects us all, where separation never exists. Of course, you can say that you *believe* in that, but to actually experience that truth in oneself requires the purest awareness—nondual awareness, the purest sense of awakening. That awakening is supported by the subtlest wind. It doesn't just happen; there is a subtle wind that supports the experience. There is a *lung*, a wind, a prana, a qi, a ch'i; you can call it a wave; you can call it a motion. There may even be ways of talking about this in scientific terms. The bottom line is that everything is connected. Does that have something to do with us? Yes. For every individual, that wave, that motion, that movement exists in us. It is a question of awakening and being connected to it. It is our ability to be aware of it that defines whether we can experience this connectedness or not. It truly is there, but whether or not we recognize it makes the difference between whether we wander in suffering or experience liberation.

Conclusion

All the meditation exercises that have been presented in this book have to do with breath. The gross breath is our inhalation and exhalation. The subtle breath has to do with awareness of the more subtle energies in the sacred body. Even simply holding a physical posture, such as the five-point posture, has something to do with the wind. The reason you place the body in various positions or move the body in certain ways is that you are trying to engage and change the wind within your body in order to support increasingly subtle awareness. The physical part of the exercise of yoga is for the purpose of influencing the wind in this way, to release the gross wind that supports disturbances and to discover the subtle wind that supports the recognition of the nature of mind. In order to experience primordial wisdom, the wind needs to become subtler and subtler.

You can try to see where you are on the map, on the list of the nine *lung*. See if you can recognize the predominant wind you may be experiencing. Of course, it may be harder to locate yourself in relation to the predominant wind that you are experiencing than it would be to find your location on the map of a state park you are exploring. Those maps are clearly drawn with different colors and markings and arrows. Unfortunately, the map of discerning inner experience is not so clearly defined. It becomes very spacious and luminous. There is so much light, but there is no red dot that says, "You are here!" It is very hard to recognize exactly where you stand, but at least each of us can try to sense where we are and where we could be headed. We have nine suggested locations on this particular map.

To summarize the journey that we have been exploring, after completing the Nine Breathings practice, you have a subtler wind from the wind you began with. Because you experience a different wind, you feel different. Because of feeling different, you have different thoughts. Because of having different thoughts, you see the world differently. Because you see the world differently, the world behaves differently toward you. You recognize opportunities to contribute and benefit others. That's how you create or change your reality. By connecting with the *lung,* you have the ability to change your perception and your reality. The chart of the nine *lung* maps out the possibilities.

JOIN THE "TRUTH OF CESSATION" CLUB

It is the cessation of anger that gives rise to love. I don't think people understand that. Most just want the fruit, love. We think we can make love appear by simply looking for it or waiting for it, but it will never come in this way. It is only the deeper truth of the release of one's anger and the subtler experience of openness in one's heart that is the good soil in which love grows. It is the cessation of sadness that leads us to experience joy. When you are aware of the conditions of pain and suffering in your life, that awareness itself is a seed. And when the naked, direct awareness of your anger or suffering allows you to release this and discover a deeper space, the more you continuously maintain clear attention to that open space in your heart, the more the seed of love grows. Space is where the infinite qualities are perfected. They manifest because what has not allowed them to manifest has been cleared. In order for them to manifest, it is necessary to rest in the truth of cessation. If you can rest in the truth of the cessation of sadness with a sense of stability, being aware of it naturally gives rise to joy. In meditation practice we train ourselves to abide, to rest without elaboration in the cessation of the blockages. We know that is the medicine. The space of cessation is the source of all the positive qualities, the antidote for whatever afflicts you. When sadness releases, joy arises. When anger releases, love is available. When prejudice releases, equanimity is present. When attachment ceases, compassion arises. Whatever the antidote, know that the seed is already there within us, and all the qualities will manifest there in the space that is revealed through the release of our preoccupation. We are not trying to do or produce anything. We simply rest in the distinctive truth of the cessation of those blockages.

I have joked with my students and invited them to join the "Truth of Cessation" Club. But truth be told, that is the only place we meet one another. That is the space within which we connect, within which we love, within which we feel like a part of the universe. The truth of cessation is the cessation of our doubt, our attachment, our aversion; and it is the great mother, the source, the union of space and awareness, the very space that is revealed the moment we release our irritation, our sadness, our desire that things be other than they are in this very moment. If you don't join the "Truth of Cessation" Club, nobody will come looking for you. But when you arrive, everyone will be waiting for you. When you arrive in the truth of cessation, you unite with everyone and all things. If you are looking for joy and you don't connect with the truth of the cessation of sadness, that is simply more sadness. So don't look in the wrong place! Joy is the natural result of the cessation of sadness. Be fearless and connect with your sadness directly and nakedly. Through the door of your very sadness, through allowing it, connecting with it, opening into and releasing it, you will discover the deeper truth of cessation and the presence of limitless joy.

If we want to make changes in our lives, we have to be willing to interrupt our all-too-familiar habitual patterns, connect with them directly, release them, and become more familiar with the opening that occurs as a result of the release of our patterns. This is something we develop over time. Can we develop this familiarity with openness with a formal two-hour meditation practice every day, or even one hour of formal practice every day? Probably we can. But many people will exclaim, "No, no, no. I am having a hard time doing it for half an hour every day. I am having a hard time just staying awake reading this book." If you forget about adding more time to your busy life, the question is, what other times are left? When is The right time to change some habits? Our Saturday morning post office meditation is one of those times. But it is not only about the post office. Start waking up and notice what occupies your mind. Perhaps there is a person who passed away in your life or a relationship that has ended and this person is still occupying a large part of your consciousness. Perhaps you have been living in an invisible position of loss and sadness. When you are walking, you are in this invisible position. You carry some sense that something is wrong, something is missing, something is not complete, something is not clear, something is not open, something is not free. You may be a living, walking, breathing example of a sense of incompleteness. But this is not your natural state. This is a habit, a product of causes and conditions that we continue to repeat, usually through the repetition of inner dialogue and through our unexamined assumptions about reality. These habits are held in our body, in our emotions, and in our mind. These habits possess a structure, a wind that can be captured and released, opening up the clear and open space of mind. The space that was once occupied by our sadness or our sense of incompleteness can be freed, and we can glimpse the deeper and truer clear and open space of being. Recognizing this space as the source of all positive qualities is the key.

Please do not misunderstand me to be saying that formal meditation practice is not important. It is very important. But you also need to look at practice slightly differently in order to bring it into everyday life. We always have time to practice. Why? Think of all the time we spend worrying. We don't need to set aside a special half-hour session for worrying, do we? No, we seem to find ample time for worrying. We are able to do it in between everything else. We can worry in the time it takes for us to reach for the door handle and step from our car. I don't know anybody who says, "I'll be right with you. I just need a little more time to worry." Why is that? Because finding time to worry is not a problem. First thing in the morning it is there. Worry doesn't follow a schedule. Standing in a line in a post office or in the bank, I can worry. In a long line for the security check at the airport, I can get agitated and have sufficient time to manifest my anxiety in creative ways. We find so much time for our habitual patterns. So in terms of a meditation practice, the time is there. You just have to recognize all those times your habitual patterns are occupying you and bring your practice to them. Join the direct awareness of your habitual pattern with your breath and release that breath in the ways we have described. When that pattern is released, you discover the truth of cessation. Abide with clear attention in the space that has opened up, in the deeper truth of cessation.

When you come to recognize and value the space that opens up, when you realize the truth of cessation, the fruit naturally arises. This is not something you believe in; this is something you experience. You do not have to do a three-year retreat to experience this, neither is this something you have to wait for the next lifetime to enjoy. If you follow these very specific instructions and bring them to the very life you are living, you will see results. Within six months of diligent exercise, you will see changes.

See what happens. Become aware of the shifts and changes you can make in your life. And when the fruit of your practice arises, share it with others. In this way, you will come to love your life and bring benefit to others in the living of your life. Your life might be simple or complex, but each of us has unique gifts to discover and contributions to make to our families, our friends, our culture, and our world. Our gifts are needed in this world. It is personally up to each one of us to make this journey of discovery, to connect with the source within us, and to allow our positive qualities to come forth. In this way, we can change our world.

ACKNOWLEDGMENTS

First, I want to thank all my teachers for their blessings and support. I am particularly grateful to Yongdzin Tenzin Namdak Rinpoche for the 40 years of loving care he has provided. Through his wisdom and love, my life has completely transformed. His blessings continuously support me to help many others.

I also want to thank all my students from many countries around the world who support the varied aspects of my work and, directly or indirectly, make my publications possible. There are too many to mention here, but I hold all of them dear in my heart.

This current publication required much work by several people whom I wish to acknowledge for the significant part they played in bringing my teachings into this present form:

Marcy Vaughn, one of my senior students, has served as the director of publications for Ligmincha Institute for many years. During that time, she has produced transcriptions of my teaching retreats and organized practice materials to support my students.

Marcy worked joyfully and rigorously on this book, gathering all my teaching on this subject from retreats I led here and abroad and, with the aid of Scott Clarwater, organizing them to capture the essential points. She edited them with a clarity and directness that make them accessible.

Rogelio Jaramillo Flores helped with the production of the accompanying online video. I am indebted to him for the many hours he spent tirelessly working on this project. Additionally, his editing of my YouTube videos has allowed my teachings to reach many around the world.

I also wish to express my appreciation to Lhari-la Kalsang Nyima for his artwork depicting the channels and chakras, his presence at Serenity Ridge, and the many ways he supports the sangha of students.

I want to thank Janine Guldener, a professional photographer from Berlin, for her generosity and kindness in producing the photographs of the *tsa lung* movements.

Sue Davis-Dill has worked hard to manage the Ligmincha Bookstore since its inception. I appreciate the many ways she has helped to make my written, video, and audio teachings available to others.

I thank Patricia Gift, my editor at Hay House, for her enthusiasm for this current project and the care and advice she offered while bringing it to fruition. Thank you also to Kendra Crossen for her excellent work copyediting and to Laura Koch and Sally Mason for all their efforts in support of this project.

To Khandro Tsering Wangmo, my wife, I am deeply grateful for the care and love she gives, not only to me and our young son, Senghe, but to the many visiting teachers and people who stay in our home, sometimes for months. She hosts them with warmth and kindness. I am grateful for her constant support of my work and her understanding when it requires me to travel away from home.

ABOUT THE AUTHOR

Tenzin Wangyal Rinpoche is an acclaimed author and teacher of students around the world. He is highly respected for his depth of wisdom, his engaging teaching style, and his ability to make ancient Tibetan teachings clear, accessible, and relevant to the lives of Westerners.

Tenzin Rinpoche is the founder and spiritual director of Ligmincha Institute, a nonprofit organization dedicated to preserving the ancient teachings, arts, sciences, language, and literature of Tibet and Zhang Zhung, the ancient kingdom associated with the Bön tradition. He is the author of *Tibetan Sound Healing; The Tibetan Yogas of Dream and Sleep; Healing with Form, Energy, and Light;* and *Wonders of the Natural Mind.* Tenzin Rinpoche resides in Charlottesville, Virginia, with his wife and son.

For more information about Tenzin Rinpoche's activities, please visit **www.ligmincha.org**.

LIGMINCHA INTERNATIONAL CENTERS

USA

LIGMINCHA INSTITUTE
Website: www.ligmincha.org
Bookstore: www.LigminchaStore.org

CHAMMA LING
Website: www.chammaling.org

HOUSTON, TX
Website: www.ligminchatexas.org

LOS ANGELES AND BERKELEY, CA
Website: ligminchaofcalifornia.com

OLYMPIA, WA
Website: www.bonpacificnorthwest.org

EUROPE

AUSTRIA
Website: www.bongaruda.at

BELGIUM
Website: www.bongaruda.be

CZECH REPUBLIC
Website: www.bongaruda.cz

DENMARK
Website: www.bongaruda.dk

FINLAND
Website: www.garudabon.fi

GERMANY
Website: www.bongaruda.de

Garuda-Berlin
Website: www.bonzentrum-berlin.de

IRELAND
Website: www.bongarudaireland.com

ITALY
Website: www.yungdrungbon.it

THE NETHERLANDS
Website: www.bongaruda.com

POLAND
Website: bongaruda.pl

RUSSIA
Website: bonpo.info

SPAIN
Website: www.bongaruda.es

SWITZERLAND
Website: www.garudaswitzerland.org

MEXICO

Website: www.garudamexico.org

BRAZIL

Website: www.bongaruda.org

Practice Groups: USA

Bön New York
M.E. McCourt
E-mail: riverwalker2@earthlink.net

Bön Philadelphia, PA
Marcy Vaughn
E-mail: marcyvaughn@msn.com

Richmond, VA
Greg Kelley
E-mail: gregckelley@hotmail.com

Practice Groups: Canada

Montreal
Maryel Sauve
E-mail: maryelsauve@mac.com

Practice Groups: Mexico

Torreon
Gaby Modero
E-mail: gabymadero9@yahoo.com.mx

Monterrey
Lourdes Hinojosa
E-mail: hinojosa_lourdes@yahoo.com

THE THREE DOORS

Transformative Practices for Body, Speech, and Mind

The Three Doors is an educational organization formed by Tibetan meditation master Tenzin Wangyal Rinpoche. It is dedicated to making selected meditation practices from the ancient Bön-Buddhist tradition available in a secular form. Its aim is to offer these practices to everyone interested in simple and direct methods that break through confusion and pain and reconnect us with qualities such as joy, love, creativity, compassion, and inner abundance, which are our birth right and essential nature.

The organization has two branches. One is an intensive three-year teachers' training program called The Three Doors Academy. The other branch offers programs for the general public, which will be taught by certified graduates of the Academy.

If you're interested in learning more, please visit our website: **www.the3doors.org**.

Bonus Content

Thank you for purchasing *Awakening the Sacred Body* by Tenzin Wangyal Rinpoche. This product includes a free streaming video! To access this bonus content, please visit www.hayhouse.com/download and enter the Product ID and Access Code as they appear below.

Product ID: 6562
Access Code: video

For further assistance, please contact
Hay House Customer Care by phone: US (800) 654-5126 or
INTL CC+(760) 431-7695 or visit www.hayhouse.com/contact.

Thank you again for your Hay House purchase. Enjoy!
Hay House, Inc. • P.O. Box 5100 • Carlsbad, CA 92018
(800) 654-5126

Awakening the Sacred Body Online Video Track List

1. Introduction

2. The Nine Breathings of Purification

3. The *Tsa Lung* Practice

4. Benefits of Practice

Caution: This video program features meditation/visualization exercises that render it inappropriate for use while driving or operating heavy machinery.

Publisher's note: Hay House products are intended to be powerful, inspirational, and life-changing tools for personal growth and healing. They are not intended as a substitute for medical care. Please use this video program under the supervision of your care provider. Neither the author nor Hay House, Inc., assumes any responsibility for your improper use of this product.

Hay House Titles of Related Interest

YOU CAN HEAL YOUR LIFE, the movie,
starring Louise Hay & Friends
(available as a 1-DVD program, an expanded 2-DVD set,
and an online streaming video)
Learn more at www.hayhouse.com/louise-movie

THE SHIFT, the movie,
starring Dr. Wayne W. Dyer
(available as a 1-DVD program, an expanded 2-DVD set,
and an online streaming video)
Learn more at www.hayhouse.com/the-shift-movie

≈ ≈ ≈

ALL YOU EVER WANTED TO KNOW
FROM HIS HOLINESS THE DALAI LAMA
ON HAPPINESS, LIFE, LIVING, AND MUCH MORE,
by His Holiness the Dalai Lama

COMMIT TO SIT: Tools for Cultivating a Meditation Practice from the
Pages of Tricycle, edited by Joan Duncan Oliver

THE FUTURE IS NOW: Timely Advice
for Creating a Better World, by His Holiness the
17th Gyalwang Karmapa, Ogyen Trinley Dorje

WHY MEDITATE?:
Working with Thoughts and Emotions,
by Matthieu Ricard

All of the above are available at your local bookstore,
or may be ordered by contacting Hay House (see next page).

We hope you enjoyed this Hay House book. If you'd like to receive our online catalog featuring additional information on Hay House books and products, or if you'd like to find out more about the Hay Foundation, please contact:

Hay House, Inc., P.O. Box 5100, Carlsbad, CA 92018-5100
(760) 431-7695 or (800) 654-5126
(760) 431-6948 (fax) or (800) 650-5115 (fax)
www.hayhouse.com® • www.hayfoundation.org

———

Published in Australia by: Hay House Australia Pty. Ltd.,
18/36 Ralph St., Alexandria NSW 2015
Phone: 612-9669-4299 • *Fax:* 612-9669-4144
www.hayhouse.com.au

Published in the United Kingdom by: Hay House UK, Ltd.,
The Sixth Floor, Watson House, 54 Baker Street, London W1U 7BU
Phone: +44 (0)20 3927 7290 • *Fax:* +44 (0)20 3927 7291
www.hayhouse.co.uk

Published in India by: Hay House Publishers India,
Muskaan Complex, Plot No. 3, B-2, Vasant Kunj, New Delhi 110 070
Phone: 91-11-4176-1620 • *Fax:* 91-11-4176-1630
www.hayhouse.co.in

———

Access New Knowledge.
Anytime. Anywhere.

Learn and evolve at your own pace
with the world's leading experts.

www.hayhouseU.com

Listen. Learn. Transform.

Listen to the audio version
of this book for FREE!

Live more consciously, strengthen your relationship with the Divine, and cultivate inner peace with world-renowned authors and teachers—all in the palm of your hand. With the *Hay House Unlimited* Audio app, you can learn and grow in a way that fits your lifestyle . . . and your daily schedule.

With your membership, you can:

- Embrace the power of your mind and heart, dive deep into your soul, rise above fear, and draw closer to Spirit.

- Explore thousands of audiobooks, meditations, immersive learning programs, podcasts, and more.

- Access exclusive audios you won't find anywhere else.

- Experience completely unlimited listening. No credits. No limits. No kidding.

Try for FREE!

Printed in the United States
by Baker & Taylor Publisher Services